SIXTY YARNS

by

Michael Toia

VOLUME I

FROG TONGUES
EDITION

Cover art by Sheila Cicchi

JOKALYM PUBLISHING
Culpeper VA

JOKALYM PRESS
Culpeper VA
K3MT@arrl.net

ISBN: 978-0-9600859-4-1

Michael Toia

To Joyce, Karen, and Lynda – my three
loves and this work's inspiration.

Introduction

Over the years I've had various experiences, and tried to relate some of the more memorable or humorous ones to my family. When my daughters reached womanhood and moved away, they requested I write these recollections, so they have some things about their father to pass on to future generations. Encouraged by them, I began a series of short notes per their wishes. This result, a sequence of short stories, I pray may be found amusing or informative by others. If it is so, my time has been well spent.

These stories were previously published as *FROG TONGUES*, ISBN 978-1-4809-3214-2. That title, curiously catchy, suggested the book dealt with the anatomy of a frog. It does not. That title did not attract those interested in short stories. This edition, *SHORT STORIES*, seeks to remedy the situation.

Contents

Michael Toia

A Girl

We three were undergraduates, in junior year, physics majors. Our cafeteria was between the engineering and science complex and the fine arts buildings. And the gym, nurse's office, and dorms were yet farther behind fine arts. We were walking along from the dorms, past fine arts, headed to the cafeteria.

Ron was the son of a professor of physics. We were discussing atomic structure and the basis for quantum mechanics found in optical spectra. Ron was ahead of us in this and most matters of physics; he had home schooling in the matter. He spoke ... we listened.

Just then the cafeteria produced a young lady, exiting, jogging lightly, quickly, down the walk, past us, farther down until the fine arts' side entrance admitted her. She wore ... well ... *nothing* much. Her garb seemed to be as a layer of black paint – an amazingly tight leotard – perfectly and completely accenting her gorgeous, 115-pound, 5'6" body that sported firm, size 'C' breasts, and an amazing derriere whose cheeks the leotard separated completely. She was in amazing shape, an example of female perfection, with a beautiful face punctuated by thin, gold hoop earrings, trailing a bouncing, blond, foot-long ponytail.

Ron continued, unfazed. We two nearly suffered whiplash! Our heads turned uncontrollably, driven by the eyes. We, so busily engaged in other matters, would have tripped over a twig or small stone had one come underfoot as we watched that voluptuous vision dance by. We missed not a second of it, and drank in all the myriad details that fascinated male college students then and now.

The vision vanished. The two of us looked at each other, exchanged amazed expressions. Ron continued, seemingly unaware of the event – for a full minute.

Then he stopped. His head slowly swiveled 180 degrees. His face took on a deeply curious, 'eureka' event look. He said, "*What* was *that?*"

We told him 'that' was what is called the female of the species, and a most alluring, perfect example thereof. One wonders how physicists manage to propagate, to keep the field going. But I assure you, in this instance, there was a two-thirds chance of it.

Michael Toia

Thespians

The weather turned warm, spring approached. It became a very nice day to be outside. I was in grad school, a part-time student and a full-time employee of the Department of Chemistry. The university excelled in science, engineering, music ... and theater.

A small band of student thespians escaped from the fine arts building and found the five broad, white, stone steps gracing the front entrance of our building. Their large, flat marble surfaces some four feet above grade, and deep runs of their stairs made an excellent area for a makeshift stage. The band began using our building, orating, in sufficient volume to be well heard.

The dean of chemistry's office was on the second floor directly above. Whole building air conditioning was, as yet, a thing of the future. The dean's windows were open to the comfortable breeze. The din became annoying, and the dean called for Al, one of his grad students.

"Al – those people are raising enough noise that I can't concentrate on my work. Go ask them to leave."

Al did. The theater band was indignant. "We have our rights! This is a free country! We have freedom of assembly! Hell, no ... we won't go!" And their volume increased.

Al reported to the dean. "They won't go, sir."

The dean said, "Al - get *rid* of them."

My small laboratory was on the third floor, directly above the area at the side of the steps occupied by the ragtag group. I was at work, my single window open, trying to ignore the commotion. Al appeared, trailing a whiff of a *terrible* stench. I ordered, "Phew! What the heck are you doing? Get out!"

Al said, "I just need your window for a second." He made it through some clutter, approached the window, stretched a hand outside, and dropped a test tube onto the stonework below. The glass broke.

In one minute, the noise abated – totally. Four more minutes and that terrible stench, fortified manifold, began wafting into my window. Fifteen minutes thereafter, the dean left for the day. Many of us in that end of the building left early that day. All was quiet on the steps. In fact, *no one* used the front entrance for several days to come.

Later I saw Al in the hallway. "What the heck *was* that stuff? And what was that all about?" Al filled me in on the entire story. He said, when the dean wanted him to 'get rid' of the group, he went to a 'fume hood' in organic chemistry, poured 1 cc of *n*-Butyl Mercaptan into a test tube, and 50 cc of acetone on top. This apparently mixed together nicely. He corked the test tube and shortly after appeared in my lab.

N-Butyl Mercaptan, I am told, is the product synthesized by skunks for their defensive spray.

Al made an entry into his lab notes.

> *1 CC N-BUTYL MERCAPTAN, 50 CC ACETONE -*
> *TOO STRONG.*
> *DILUTE ABOUT 50:1. EFFECTIVE FOR CROWD*
> *DISPERSAL.*

As one proceeds through life, one learns from experiences. The wise have learned not to trifle with, or rankle, certain people, who can exact a vengeful payback. Chemists, for example.

Michael Toia

Alice

We've lived together, husband and wife, lover and lovee, for many a year. She has always been rather frugal with what I can provide. I, on the other hand, simply send my earnings into our mutual checking account. This arrangement has served the two of us well for so many decades.

She is not an avid coupon clipper, but she is a careful shopper. If a product is on the shelf, or advertised for sale, and she sees only a slight possibility of needing it, the item remains unsold. But if there, put on a two-for-one sale, a pair of them will appear in our house. I believe that, to her, it is the thrill of the hunt.

She uses credit cards wisely. One or more of them offers airline miles. When I returned home one evening, she announced that she had sufficient points so we could fly off to a nice vacation, and she had it planned out.

I am lousy at planning vacation trips. She, on the other hand, has taken us to some awesome places: Puerto Rico, Saints Croix/Thomas/Johns, Bermuda, Bahamas, Mexico, Canada, and many, many places in the US. Her plans always resulted in a most relaxing, interesting, and memorable trip … and this was no exception.

She took me to Alice … Alice Springs; the Outback … the center of Australia.

We prepared. It occurred to me that our digital camera had but one battery, and it was a few years old. It could likely croak during the trip, and we would have no photos for our album. I looked over the Internet, and found how to order replacements. I wanted to buy two more. However, they were not in stock. I order a pair, but was assured they would not arrive in time for the trip.

So, I packed my trusty Pentax, and bought a dozen rolls of Ektachrome film, as I had done so many times in the pre-digital camera era. With the Pentax, I planned on photo-documenting our vacation.

Now, Alice is a really nice spot to visit. We thoroughly enjoyed it. The only problem is transportation: you must sit in an airplane for seventeen hours to go from the USA to Australia. That is a bit of a drag, and hard on the legs, etc. And, they will not let you stay in Australia, so you must do the same to get back home, but it was worth it.

We, unfortunately, did NOT have enough time to take the side trip to Ayers Rock. But I, as a dedicated radio telegraph operator, did really enjoy the visit to the Overland Telegraph Museum at Alice, formerly a major relay station on the line linking Darwin to Adelaide.

The camera was put to good use, and many photos resulted. I shot all the film I had taken, and bought more as well. We photographed most of Alice, and a lot of Melbourne as we stayed a few days at each.

Now came the return trip, that seventeen-hour flight back to the States, and five more to our home city. There was the time change of about twelve hours as well, so we rested for a few days, allowing our biological clocks time to re-synchronize to the sun again, halfway 'round the globe.

We wanted to get our photography processed, but ran into problems. It seems I am a fossil from a bygone era; one-hour MotoPhoto doesn't do Ektachrome anymore. Nor does the local photo counter at the drug store, Walmart, or any other place I tried.

So, I thought, *it's up to me*. Years ago I did wet chemistry photo processing, and bought chemical kits from industrial photo supply houses to process Ektachrome. I've done over 4,000 slides of all my family photography in several decades.

Alas, I could find neither my film processing tanks and equipment, nor a supply house that carried those chemicals anymore. What do to? What to do?

Finally, after calling around quite a bit, I found a photo shop that *did* Ektachrome. What a relief; we could finally get our photos. I went to the shop, and talked to a man across the counter. I said, "I'm told you process Ektachrome film?"

He said, "Yeah … we do all sorts of special stuff. We even do daguerreotypes!"

- - - ! - - -

AXX12

We had just stood down from the Cuban Missile Crisis. Lessons learned put many Army units on various training missions; we were no exception.

In that day, worldwide communication by satellite was on the theoretical planning boards, cell phones were still fifteen years yet to come, and world-spanning fiber cable systems would not appear for a few decades. Very long distance intercontinental communiaation was done by shortwave radio. Our function was to operate one such radio terminal.

We were given the mission of establishing a training 'shot,' a two-way radio link between our base in the state of Georgia, and another similar unit near Orleans, France. These radio waves bounce off a sort of mirror some distance above the earth, called the ionosphere. This mirror's reflectivity varies depending on how much sunlight hits it, and how active the sun happens to be. To effect the radio link, we had to shift operating frequencies between daytime and nighttime on a scheduled basis, and to track the similar changes made by Orleans.

We were able to 'copy' Orleans shortly after the exercise began, but could not get them to acknowledge our signal. We transmitted a conglomerate of one voice channel and sixteen radio teletype channels. The teletype channels all carried a standard 'FOX' message:

THE QUICK BROWN FOX JUMPED OVER THE LAZY DOGS BACK 1234567890 RYRYRYRYRYRY

line after monotonous line, using all twenty-six letters of the alphabet, the ten numeric digits, and a sequence of 'RYs', known as *reversals* because of their specific coded structure. When copying FOX, it is easy to look at the paper from hours of reception, hundreds of lines making a quilt-like pattern, and spot errors, because the pattern down each page is so uniform.

Our voice channel carried a short voice message:

THIS IS US ARMY RADIO STATION AXX12 FORT WHATZIT GEORGIA TRANSMITTING FOR STATION IDENTIFICATION AND RECEIVER TUNING.

again, one monotonous drone after another, at about one-minute intervals, in the voice of some gruff-sounding sergeant. Two days went by, and Orleans did not acknowledge our transmissions.

On the third day, the Officer in Charge – the OIC – brought his sweetheart to the equipment, and had *her* read, then speak, the voice message. This he recorded, and on the third try said, "Perfect! Thank you, darling." She departed for the commissary – PX – and her usual daily rounds.

I did say we were located in Georgia. Well, the OIC's wife, nee a Yankee, had developed that beautiful, honey-dripping, female Georgia accent that I find impossible to describe in print. It was the same text as above, but at about half-cadence. Her voice had an amazingly 'come hither,' yet at the same time, sweetly innocent quality that could melt a stone. I let you, the reader, try to imagine the sound ... and, no matter how hard you try, you will still fall short of reproducing it.

We put the newly recorded message in place of the original. In five minutes Orleans had copy on us. It just takes the proper incentive.

The mission continued for a month. With two-way copy, we took four of our sixteen teletype channels off of FOX and began exchanging practice messages. Real messages related to the operation of the equipment and some personal comments were also interjected with the practice material as we saw fit. And, some of them began to come back from Orleans:

"Who is that gal?"

"What's her address and telephone number?"

"I'm coming stateside next month. How can I make a date with her?"

More proposals of dates, and a few of marriage, came across the radio link!

To entertain the troops overseas, the OIC picked out a picture of this beautiful creature, in a then-very interesting two-piece striped bikini, took it to the photo lab, and had an enlargement made. As we had facilities to transmit facsimile over our voice channel, the photo went 'on the air.' It was, well, well received … indeed!

The operation came to an end. We never let the air out of the fantasy balloon, and never told the other end that the 'pinup gal' was the OIC's *wife*. We just did not have the heart to do it. And for many a year, *he* never told *her* about it, either.

The Clock

The family attributes my scientific aptitude to my father. He nurtured me when I was young, encouraged my curiosity into all things technical, and insisted I attend the local university to study engineering. We lived nine miles from Carnegie Mellon, then known as '*Carnegie Tech.*'

You had to know my father. I loved him very much. A master machinist, instrument maker, auto mechanic, and jeweler, he was acknowledged as one of the very best in his trade. No mechanical system, however delicate, was beyond his ability, which leads us to *the clock*.

While pursuing an advanced degree at Carnegie, I had a colleague, a friend named Pli, who had come from Paris. There he had purchased a most interesting clock, a *LeCoultre Atmos*. This was in the day preceding electronic timepieces, and *the clock* was a mechanical wonderment, never needing to be wound, never needing batteries or other apparent energy source. It wound its mainspring by a temperature-sensitive mechanism – a one degree Fahrenheit change in either direction in one day would impart enough energy to keep its delicate oscillating mechanism running.

The clock refused to run for more than several days at a time. Pli had taken it to a number of repair facilities at stores that marketed the LeCoultre product. No one could get it to run for more than a few weeks.

In exasperation one day, he said, "Where can one find a good clock repairman?"

I said, "I know the best in the area, the best in several counties. But I warn you ... I am prejudiced ... he is my father."

Well, I introduced father and Pli. They became very close friends. By and by, the *clock* was brought to father to see what he might do.

To shorten the story, father *did* repair it, and it ran in his shop for several months. Pli would visit mother and father most weekends, and they welcomed him with warmth and a good meal. He always brought wine, a type my parents really favored. He would see his clock in father's shop and ask about it.

Finally, father said, "It's been running continuously for six months. I'm satisfied that it is, in fact, repaired. Take it with you." And Pli did.

The three-way friendship – mother, father, and Pli – continued unabated. Two years later Pli was transferred to the West Coast. He spoke to father about it, saying, "*The clock* will likely not survive the trip. I want to give it to you as a present, for your years of friendship."

Father had a strong sense of doing right, would never take advantage of anyone, and his pride. He refused the gift. But Pli also had pride. I am told they came to some agreement or other, and father *did* acquire *the clock*. It occupied a position of prominence in the family living room from 1967 to 1975, and never once skipped a beat. Thereafter it became an ornament, until mother bequeathed it to me in 1995. It is still in my possession.

However, there is an amazing story yet to be told ...

Father was an enormous fan of Harry Houdini, the famous escape artist. Houdini, we were reminded several times a year, had made a pact with his wife that, were it possible to contact the living from the world beyond, she was to be especially attentive exactly one year after Harry's death ... he would try to contact her. I do not know of the result, but Father insisted that, one year after *his* death, Mother do the same.

Father passed away at 3:15 A.M. on August 23, 1974.

I had moved to Maryland, and my phone rang at 6 A.M. August 23. It was Mother. She was distraught. I asked, "What's wrong? Are you all right?"

She said she had been deeply depressed, this being the first anniversary of Father's death. She had been unable to sleep at all that night. She had gone to the kitchen to get yet another cup of coffee.

While sitting at the table, she noticed the first light of dawn. She went to check the time. She looked at *the clock*. It read ... **3:15 A.M.**

But it was dawn! What had happened?

It was *the clock*. It had stopped!

Mother was truly spooked. I was amazed! I sat up in bed and shouted, "He *DID* it!"

Mother activated *the clock's* storage mechanism. It never ran in her house again. I begged her to give, or sell, it to me. For years she refused, knowing full well that I intended to put it back in service, and see if father could communicate via it to me. I am an accomplished Morse code radio operator, and father knew that. However, I did acquire *the clock* a few short years before mother passed away.

It once again will not run continuously. I have examined it in detail, yet have not been able to make it run for longer that about three weeks. This is the state in which it rested when father first looked at it. When he got it running, I asked, "What was wrong? How did you fix it?"

He said, "I'll not tell you. But someday you will look at it when it gets to the stopping state again. You are my son. You will be able to see the problem and repair it."

But my wife is also seemingly spooked by it, as every time I think about getting it to run, she tries to discourage me. I would *love* to get it going again, but the love of my dear wife is stronger, so it sits in storage at my home. Our younger daughter, a mechanical engineer, is interested in acquiring it and, perhaps it will be *she* who completes the messaging medium.

Could it be? Love ya, Father.

Fearless

In my undergraduate years I worked part time as an electronic technician in the university chemistry department. After graduation and two years service with the Army, I became a government civilian in a research laboratory.

One day a letter arrived from my former university boss. It explained that his research engineer, who did the electronic stuff, had moved on. They needed a replacement. Would I be interested? So by and by the department had a new engineer, and the position offered half tuition. By that route, I earned a master's degree in physics, though employment was in chemistry. Many of my friends were organic chemistry grad students.

The time was the late 1960s. Air conditioning would be along years later. And, on a September day, a small band of 'hippie peaceniks' had a makeshift stage and podium on the campus mall. The Vietnam War was being hotly protested. Buddhist monks were self-immolating on streets in Asian cities. Peaceniks were agitating against the war.

It was a warm day with a gentle breeze. Morning wore on, and the student body began to assemble and spread out across the grass. The crowd grew more and more dense. Needing to cross the mall, I found it tricky to pick the way carefully, so as not to step on fingers, arms, legs, or other assorted body parts. Peaceniks continued to speak through their bullhorns. Tension seemed to build – the air became more and more electric. I stood just outside my lab building, a safe distance from the crowd, ready to dive through and lock the door behind me. The university president was apprised of the situation and a staff member suggested calling police. He wisely assessed that their presence would catalyze a riot.

From later talk among the faculty, I presume the following:

The university president called the dean of chemistry. Not long after, two tall, hulky beings emerged from the bowels of the chemistry building, up the outside steps, and approached the edge of the mall. Each carried a long pole, taken from the lecture hall, their usual purpose to open and close the upper bays of windows.

The beings separated, holding their poles upright. Between them was a paper banner, made of a dozen feet of 132-column "Z" fold computer paper common in those times. The banner contained a hastily-drawn, but clearly readable message.

They picked their way carefully, slowly through the crowd, approaching the podium, stood before it for a minute, exposing the banner to the peaceniks. Then they came about, and displayed the banner to the crowd.

A wave of light laughter sprang up. Mirth spread. In short order, the audience developed a profound laugh, then began to walk off … the crowd thinned, then slowly disappeared.

The duo was from chemical engineering. Even before that day and well beyond, I held these types to be the world's most fearless people – their job being manufacture of tank-car lots of nitro-glycerin, shiploads of ammonium nitrate, huge quantities of sulfuric acid, ten million gallon lots of aviation gasoline, and so forth.

The banner's message?

IF YOU ARE TRULY SERIOUS, BURN YOURSELVES

Michael Toia

Fast forward now many years. My family was vacationing in the Northwest. Staying in Idaho Falls, we visited a museum site at the Idaho National Engineering Laboratories, the site of 'EBR-1,' Experimental Breeder Reactor number one. There, circa 1951-52, nuclear physicists became nuclear power engineers: they had constructed and operated a prototype nuclear power plant.

Study of the displays and placards revealed how it worked. A nuclear reactor heated a metal fluid that then was pumped through a boiler, producing quality steam that in turn spun a turbine. An electric generator then produced power to light the building and its small complex.

I mused: "Let's see ... these people used an atomic bomb that they detonated very carefully, to heat a ton or so of liquid metal, called NaK, an alloy of sodium (Na) and potassium (K) that is liquid at room temperature. It won't freeze in the pipes.

"This, they passed through steel pipes into a boiler, where the NaK yielded its heat to produce steam, and dropped in temperature.

"They re-circulated the cooled, liquid NaK to the bomb, where it was re-heated.

"The steam then drove a turbine, which spun the generator.

"Interesting."

Well! Then I remembered something from my chemistry classes. What would happen if that sodium leaked into the water? BOOM! It would immediately produce hydrogen gas and great heat. The gas explodes! And potassium does the same, with greater vigor!

So that day, I concluded, "Move over, chem engineers. You are brave and fearless, indeed. But these nuclear power engineers beat you by a country mile. *They* are the world's most fearless people.

Hammer

MY undergraduate years were 1955 to 1960. By most standards, I was a committed member of 'geekdom.' Even before college, I obtained a *ham radio* license, and in college was a member of the ham radio club. The personal computer was *years* off.

Our club 'shack,' as amateur radio stations are called, was on the fourth and top level of 'machinery hall,' which housed the electrical engineering department. The club's faculty advisor was none other than the department head, one Dr. Williams, to whom I owe a debt of thanks: he refused my later entry to grad school in his department, forcing me to beg my way into the physics department, where I later earned an advanced degree. I now make a living knowing a tad about radio antennas, where we shake electrons to make radio waves. But I digress. I run ahead of myself.

In our undergrad days, Dr. Williams encouraged us to *build*, from scratch, a radio transmitter to operate at the maximum power allowed by FCC regulations. And, we began.

I tackled the part of the transmitter that generates a low power radio signal and imparts modulation onto it; that is, it produces a weak radio signal that has all the information we want to transmit, whether voice or Morse, and just needed something to amplify its power level.

Another chap or two took on the design of the power amplifier, and my good former friend Dick, took on the task of building the 4,000-volt supply that would power the amplifier.

Dick's design included a motor-driven variable transformer, permitting us to change the voltage to anything from zero to the full 4,000 volts. He worked on it most lunch hours, and I, on my piece of the whole. Because of the immense weight of the several transformers – big, hunky assemblages of copper and steel – the power supply would be the lowest level of a metal tower that would house the entire transmitter.

I worked on a big, machinist-type heavy oak bench, and Dick worked while squatting or kneeling on the floor.

He worried for days about the variable transformer. It had a little motor on it and a big gear, about a foot in diameter, that the motor would drive through a tiny gear, to adjust the output voltage.

Each day over a few weeks, he would carefully measure the position of the gear, using a hand-held 'multimeter' instrument that we used in the day. He was sure he had it set to the minimum, zero-output voltage position, but worried about it daily nonetheless.

Now, Dick had prepared a small remote control box with a RED and BLACK button on it. Pressing the former would turn the transformer ON, and the latter OFF. Finally came the day that he wired the monster transformer to the power mains. All was now ready for its first 'Power Up' test. He nervously looked at it, again, and again. I watched.

Finally, he screwed up his courage, and cautiously, hesitatingly, reached toward the RED button. I watched. I picked up a large, 3-pound, ball peen hammer.

As he hit the button, I mercilessly whacked the hammer down on that oak bench. The result was amazingly funny! Dick seemed to jump right out of his skin! I roared with laughter.

Dick did not. He glared at me – menacingly – with one thought in his mind ... KILL! I never saw a man's face turn so red, before nor since. I now realized that, although convulsed in mirth, I might be in deep doodoo. I dropped the hammer on the bench and made a very quick exit.

Dick came right after me, BUT HE HAD PICKED UP THE HAMMER! I was truly in a state of possible maximum hurt.

I took the twelve steps to the inter-floor landing, three at a time, spun about the landing, and took the additional twelve steps to the third floor in like manner. But so did Dick! And his words did not instill confidence in me, or anyone else in the area. They did stoke the flight response.

I spun around the stairwell, and started taking four steps at a time, around the next landing, continuing in like manner to the second, then the first, and main floor, shot down the main hall to the opposite end of the building, and down the enormous facade of steps leading to the campus mall. Dick was never more than about two arms length from me the whole time. I was still somewhat convulsed with mirth, tinged by a good helping of abject fear. Dick was still operating on that overdose of adrenaline that I had catalyzed.

About three hundred feet along the mall, I tripped. Dick pounced on me. e proceeded to beat the !@#$ out of me. I found it impossible to fight back, as we were earlier close friends.

Finally, his adrenaline wore down. looked at me. said, "What have I done?"

I said, "I don't know, but I don't feel too good. n you help me to the nurse's office?"

We got to the school nurse. I had two black eyes, bruises all over my face, was bleeding from my nose, and both ears were quite black and blue. The nurse asked, "What in the world happened to you?"

I said, "My friend here beat the dickens out of me."

Now, at the time I weighed about 190 pounds and stood 5'11", and Dick may have weighed all of about 130, at about 5'6". The nurse didn't believe me, but I opined I had really earned the beating. The next day someone turned the hammer in to the electrical engineering office. They found it midway along the first floor, or else this story would need to be related by Dick, as I simply would not be here.

Strangely, a few days later I was well enough to show my battered face on campus. I encountered Dick. He was an amazing fella. We were still friends.

Michael Toia

Heat

My hometown was basically an armed camp. Every household had at least one deer rifle, and most, an assortment of handguns, shotgun, etc. Their children learned to respect guns at an early age. Many of us fired our first rifle at about age four or so. You would expect this environment to produce a type of mayhem with gunfire in all directions.

Such was not the case. I cannot recall more than one incident in my years there involving a firearm injury and that was the shooting death of the chief of police when he went to answer a call of domestic violence. The burglary and robbery rate was, as far as I can recall, nil. Criminals are not stupid.

My wife, on the other hand, was reared in a loving home where never was a firearm permitted. I do not know much about her neighborhood to comment on crime rate, but it was not notorious. As far as I can say, the crime rates in the two towns were probably about the same, leading one to conclude that presence or absence of guns has little effect thereupon.

We were wed. We rented a small cottage in an adjoining state. When I returned from work one evening early in our married life, my love was alarmed. She exclaimed excitedly, "There's a gun in that closet! The people who lived here before must have forgotten it!" I looked. "Ahhhh ... this is mine. It's a .22-caliber, single-shot Winchester rifle, given to me as my own, by my father on my ninth birthday. I've had it ever since." And, I still do.

My bride was a bit taken aback, so I arranged that the coming weekend, we would go out to a local sand borrow pit, or quarry, and show her how the rifle works. I bought a box of 50 rounds of .22 longs, and that weekend we did just as planned. She became far less frightened of the thing, and actually began to see that sport shooting can be fun.

I drilled into her the basic four rules of firearm safety:

1. Never put your finger on the trigger until you are ready to shoot.

2. A gun will immediately load itself at any time you put it down. When you pick it up, it is ready to fire. Your first priority is to 'clear' it.

3. Don't ever point a gun at anything you do not intend to kill or destroy.

4. Be sure of your target, and everything between and beyond.

Later in life, we moved onto a snake-infested farm. The trusty .22 was just not up to the task of taking on the reptile population, so we acquired a .410 shotgun. That did the trick. In a few short years it dispatched many a snake, at the rate of a half-dozen or so a week.

Then we moved back to city life. Reagan and Brady were shot in an assassination attempt. Public fervor by some brought about the 'Brady Bill.'

The following October, my sweet asked me to take her to a nearby town, which I did. On arriving, she presented me a two-column-inch newspaper ad for a local gun store, and said, "Can you take me there?"

I said, "Let's see ... but just what do you have in mind?"

She replied, "I'm going to buy you a Christmas present. I want you to pick out a pistol of your choice."

"Why?" said I.

"It's the law," said she. "One gun a month."

What? *She* would buy *me* a pistol? I didn't believe it. However, we found the store, and soon thereafter I was the happy owner of a Smith and Wesson .38 Special, a gun I had admired since seeing one the first time. We proceeded to the store's range and tried it out. It's a really nice piece.

Some years later, I was out of town on business again. During one of my nightly phone calls, my sweets allowed as to how the burglar alarm had gone off in the middle of the night, and gave her a good fright. I'm told she called the police, and then pushed the family dog from room to room. The dog just yawned and looked at her. Had there been an intruder, the dog was the type that would likely have drawn blood. My sweets carried the Smith and Wesson with her.

Then she confided, "I have a confession to make. I slept the rest of the night with your .38 Special under my pillow."

DANG! DO I HAVE A SPECIAL GAL OR NOT? I'M PROUD OF HER. She went from a family with no firearms at all, to our little love nest that has a tiny arsenal with several hundred rounds of ammunition to match our small collection of guns.

But, note to self: The next time she says, "Not tonight, I have a headache," check under the pillow!

She did not buy me one gun each month, but did buy me a few more in the following years. And she insisted that I have a 'concealed carry' permit. No wonder I love that woman.

Santa

One October evening, we visited a fellow parishioner who was quite ill. He was sleeping. We sat in the living room talking with his wife. The kitchen door opened, admitting three more people – his daughter, son-in-law, and 4-year-old granddaughter Ellie.

Ellie came bounding toward Grandma, saw us, stopped dead in her tracks, and ran back to Daddy. He came to the doorway, Ellie attached firmly to, and behind, his leg. She would venture a shy peek from time to time.

Somewhat later, I took my 250-pound frame to the kitchen for a bit of water. Ellie, Dad, and Mom were sitting at the table. She looked intently and apprehensively at me. I turned to her, gave her a wink, stroked my grey beard, and teased, "It gets a lot longer soon. It grows real fast. I bet you didn't expect to see Santa here, did you?" And that ignited magic that went along these lines, to the best of my recollection.

• • • • •

Ellie (after a thoughtful pause): Do you have flying deer?

Me: "Oh no. Deer don't fly. You mean *Reindeer*."

Ellie (wide eyed): "They *fly*?"

Me (index finger over lips): "Shhh ... that's a secret."

Ellie: "A secret?"

Me: "Of course. If people knew for sure, I'd have to get license plates for all the reindeer, and that would cost a lot of money. Besides, I only use them once a year."

There was a pause. The adults chatted a bit, then there came a tug on my right sleeve. It was Ellie, and I bowed down to listen.

Ellie: "Are you really Santa Claus?"

Me: "I'm one of them."

Ellie: "One of them?"

Me: "Why sure. We're all cousins, uncles ... a big family. When Saint Nicholas started being Santa, he just covered Scandinavia, and there weren't as many children then, too. They loved him, so he had to have his brothers and cousins help out."

Ellie: "Do you have a sleigh?"

Me: "Uh huh. Not like the old ones, though. Now we have computers to help us check our routes, find our way, and make sure we don't skip any children. We even have sleigh-to-sleigh phones and a direct line to Santa Central at the North Pole, too."

Ellie: "Do you come to my house?"

Me: "Gee, I don't have my computer with me. I'd have to check. But I think you're on my cousin Sidney's route, not mine. I'm mostly East of here."

I went back to the living room and stood there listening to more adult chit-chat. Shortly, another tug and a bow as Ellie left her daddy and came over to me.

Ellie: (munching slowly on a cookie): "Do you come down the chimney?"

Me: "Sometimes – only if there isn't a fire in the fireplace!

Michael Toia

But we have other secret ways to come into children's houses."

Ellie: "You *do*?"

Me: "We have to. Some houses don't have chimneys. We can't forget those children, can we?"

Yet more adult chatter, then another tug and a bow.

Ellie: "Are the elves making toys now?"

Me: "Why, of course. They do all year long."

Ellie: "All year?"

Me: "Yes. We can't make all the toys overnight, or in a week. Besides, if the elves didn't work all year, what would they do? I'd have to lay them off. They'd have to go on welfare. So we work the whole year, and have lots of fun working, too … making toys. We have to test them, too, to make sure they work okay, and that's a lot of fun."

Some of us went to Granddad's bedroom. We took turns talking to him at bedside. Then came another tug and a bow. It was Ellie. She had broken her cookie in two, and offered me half.

Me: "Oh, thank you, sweetheart. But cookies have lots of sugar in them. I'm not allowed to eat too much sugar because I'm diabetic. You go ahead and eat my half, too. But it was so lovely of you to offer."

Ellie: "But if you can't eat cookies, what happens to them when we put them near the tree for Santa?"

Me: "Oh, I shouldn't eat cookies, but I do on Christmas Eve. I love them. Besides, I have eight reindeer and they love cookies, too. So I share them with my reindeer."

Ellie: "What about Rudolph? Isn't he one of your reindeer?"

Me: "Rudolph goes on the foggy routes. I use him only when it's foggy. He helps a lot of us, because while we're coming down the chimney, he goes off to guide another sleigh."

Ellie: "All over the world?"

Me: "No, just here. I'm called Santa Claus here. But not in Canada."

Ellie: "What do they call you there?"

Me: "Why, Pere Noel, of course. It's French. It means 'Father Christmas.' I think my cousins in France are called Pere Noel, too. Rudolph's cousins have different names in different parts of the world, too."

Ellie sank into deep thought. I think she was drinking it all in, trying to soak it up. We continued with a bit more adult chatter. Then there was a pat on my belly. I bowed again.

Ellie: "Your tummy is round like Santa."

Me: "Of course. And when I put on my heavy red coat over a few sweaters, I look much rounder, just like you do when you put on your winter coat!"

We had more adult chatter, some of it about Ellie's reactions to me, and mine to her. Finally, it was time to leave. We went to the kitchen and put on our coats, and said goodbye to our hostess.

And then the magic peaked. Ellie came over to me, threw her arms around my tummy, as far as they would reach, and gave me a good, really earnest hug. I ran my hand down over her beautiful red hair, bent down, returned her hug, and kissed her on the head.

I had an experience I shall take to the grave. It is sad Ellie will too soon discover that I'm just an eccentric old humbug. But her Mom tells us, she's convinced she talked to Santa that night.

That's good enough for me.

Skibo

Our school cafeteria was, is, and likely always will be, called "Skibo" after Andrew Carnegie's Scottish castle. The year was 1955. I entered Carnegie Tech. Skibo was housed in an old, World War I-style aircraft hanger, probably about three hundred feet deep, a high roof center bay about a hundred feet wide, and two lower roof side bays, each about fifty feet wide. It was poorly lit, but constantly occupied. There were several card games going on at all times, as students entered, left to attend classes, and returned.

We loved Skibo. It was the de facto student union. But it was OLD ... too old ... and too dim. The side windows of the center bay would admit occasional sunlight, though they had probably not been washed for years. Perhaps they were of aging glass, more translucent than transparent. You must remember we were only a few miles from several steel mills, and grimy windows were common.

Occasionally someone would order soup. On a hot fall day, I looked into mine. There was a long, thin, black hair floating on it! Gross! I fished it out, wiped my spoon on a napkin. I was too poor to throw the soup out, and college students eat darned near anything, so I continued. My friends had a bit of a laugh about me.

What! There was another hair in my soup – more like on it, floating on the surface. I fished it out, too. We could not believe it: The soup du jour seemed to be hair soup. And another appeared as we watched. In fact, it surfaced gradually, lengthening by the minute. What was this stuff?

We looked toward the dim ceiling and behold! There seemed to be a very thin cobweb hanging down from the roof some tens of feet above. In fact, the diffused sunlight revealed many strands of cobweb, all over the entire cafeteria. They were hair thin, not strong, and as people walked about, they simply broke off, adhered to their clothes, and were so light and thin that they were unnoticeable.

Cobwebs? Is the place infested with nests of spider under the roof? And, aren't spider webs rather strong?

They were very thin lines of roofing tar! When the roof was warmed by the sun, its tar oozed slowly through the roof planks and began a slow descent to the floor, extruding into those very fine hair-like strands.

The university decided the building had to go, and a wealthy benefactress donated a considerable sum to build a new library building. Skibo was an excellent site, and the new library later sat, or perhaps still, sits there.

Our beloved and venerated Skibo was slated for closure and demolition. The announcement was akin to being told that your dog has rabies! The timetable was announced, and on its final week, circa 1959, Skibo hosted a week-long party. On the last day, a local, famous disk jockey came and spent the afternoon entertaining us.

His current female companion accompanied him. She was, I am told, very nice on the eyes. Some of the male student body recognized her. She was a stripper at the downtown burlesque house! It did not take long for this news to shoot through the crowd, and even less time for the male contingent to begin chanting, "Take it off! Take it off! Take it off!"

Well, the young lady was flattered by this response. Some assisted her to the top of a table, while others cleared it off. She began her burlesque routine, slowly, teasingly removing one article of clothing after another.

The place erupted in howls of approval, whistles, more chanting, and chanting of burlesque music to accompany her. Before she could complete her routine, the city police arrived. They raided the place! The stripper and her DJ friend were quickly escorted out a rear door by some very appreciative students and faculty.

Skibo went out in grand style, and its final party made the local papers.

V2

Florida's Space Coast is always worth a visit. I've been there on business many a time. On occasion my sweetheart likes to come along, and I delight in her presence. After all, our two children are products of Florida, having been born way, way up in the panhandle at Chipley. The state has a special meaning to us.

Not long ago, I attended a conference at Patrick Air Force Base. The last day was an optional tour of Canaveral Air Force Station, where the early sub-orbital and orbital flights were launched, in the pre-Cape Kennedy era. There is a lot of history on this installation. My sweetie was along on that trip.

This visit occurred shortly after a few of the original launch control buildings were opened to the public as a museum. One had been the control facility for the Mercury astronaut program. The building is not overly large, but was sufficient for the purpose.

Entry was to a main area, the centerpiece of which was a German V2 rocket engine. An ever-curious engineer, I busied myself examining it in great detail. My darling tagged along, humoring me.

She said, "Isn't this one of Von Braun's?"

I said, "No, this is the World War II German V2. Von Braun didn't come here until after the war."

She said, "Wasn't Von Braun German?"

- - - ! - - -

Of course, and this specific piece of equipment may well have been plumbed by Von Braun himself!

Chalk up one for the wife ... she got me!

Michael Toia

Tuna

Late October, 1962, the Cuban Missile Crisis was in full swing. My communications unit was slated to deploy on classified orders, but our maintenance had been sorely lacking for several years. It was deemed we should instead be attached to the post Signal Field Maintenance facility, and their orders were to bring us up to full operability as soon as possible. The facility had several civilians, one a retired colonel who told the following story. I had not heard it earlier nor have I since, and I have forgotten the colonel's name. Its attribution remains 'anon.'

- - - - -

Jake, a died-in-the-wool fisherman, spoke of his experience on a deep sea fishing vacation he had taken. The charter boat made it out to the fishing grounds, and everyone aboard got into the action. Jake hooked a large fish. He fought it. It fought back. The crew coached him on how to work the fish – reel in – give him some slack – reel in. He fought that fish for hours. At times it jumped completely out of the water. My gosh! It was a sailfish! Must have weighed a thousand pounds! So claimed Jake.

Cleo, also an avid fisherman, listened, emoting to Jake's experience, almost feeling them himself. But alas! Jake just could not land that fish, so after about five hours, and now at exhaustion, he had no choice other than to cut it loose. But, a thousand pound sailfish! What an experience! Cleo then related a similar experience. He and his friend Joe had gone to Florida on a similar deep sea fishing vacation, and spent a week there.

On Wednesday they signed on to a charter boat and sailed out to the skipper's favorite fishing grounds. Everyone got to it, and began fishing. They landed a number of fish, too.

Jake nodded in agreement.

Cleo then hooked a tuna, a big one. It fought back, hard, and Cleo also had a time of it landing that fish. But, land it, he did. Magnificent!

What a fish! The biggest he had ever caught, by far.

Now, what does one do with a big fish, especially when on vacation? Take it home? Impractical, to say the least. Dockside the charter company had a photographer with the proper setup, and one could buy a photograph of his big catch. Cleo did just that.

His tuna was weighed in at 235 pounds; not the world's largest, but Cleo's largest. After the weigh-in and photograph, Cleo took advantage of another of the company's options – he signed his tuna over to a local fish processing plant. The plant guaranteed to return to anyone so doing, ten percent of the processed fish, canned and ready to take home. Cleo thought this to be a wise option.

Jake nodded.

Cleo and Joe returned to their hotel, had a bit of supper, still excited about the day, and retired to the cocktail lounge. While relaxing and having a drink or two, watching a game on the lounge TV, Cleo was paged: he had a telephone call. Seemed the foreman on night shift at the fish cannery was calling; said there was something unusual about Cleo's tuna. He explained that these fish browse the ocean, encounter all sorts of junk, and the plant often finds old boots, license plates, beer bottles, and such in their gullet. They found something of possible value in Cleo's tuna, and wanted to know if he could come by and decide what to do about it.

Michael Toia

Well, neither Cleo nor Joe had been inside a fish processing plant, and had nothing important to do, and both their curiosities were really aroused. The foreman gave Cleo instructions on how to find the place, and off they went in their rental car. They found their way.

They approached the door the foreman had told them to use, tapped on it, and shortly the foreman himself admitted them. He led them to his small office. On his desk sat the object of the foreman's query. It was encrusted in barnacles, rather corroded, but obviously made of a decent quality brass, with the concomitant 'heft.' What the heck was it?

Jake's look turned to a mix of anticipation and disbelief.

The foreman said he had tried to clean it up a bit, trying to identify it, but he didn't have much time, or the right materials. Cleo and Joe went off to an all-night drug store. They bought some Brasso, a few Blitz cloths, some other metal cleaning fluid, and a few small cleaning rags. They found some light-grade sandpaper and added it to their order. Then they returned to the foreman's desk.

Cleo worked on the object carefully. It was from his fish, after all, and rightfully his. Carefully sanding off the barnacles, applying the cleaning fluid, working with a sense of passionate curiosity, he continued. What was this object?

Jake's expression continued as previously, but growing in disbelief.

Finally the object was rather well cleaned, down to its polished brass surface. Good grief! It was an old ship's oil lamp, like those used centuries ago by the Spanish galleons that sailed these waters. It must have fallen overboard during a storm or such. And there it sat ... Cleo's very own possession!

Jake objected, claimed Cleo was telling a typical fish story, a lie, and a whopper at that. Nonetheless, Cleo wasn't finished with his tale. Quiet down ... be patient ... let him continue.

Cleo did. It appeared there might be an inscription of some sort on the lamp, dim, not immediately legible. However, after carefully working on it, he finally realized it read, "The Santa Maria!"

The Santa Maria! My word! Imagine! We know Columbus sailed these waters, and history tells us he did get caught in a storm. probably got caught in more than one. This very lamp, from the Santa Maria, fell overboard, sat on the ocean floor, this tuna ingested it, and here it was, on the foreman's desk ... Cleo's to have and to hold.

Jake howled in protest! Preposterous! A giant fish tale! A fabrication! A whopper!

But Cleo said hold on, he wasn't done yet. There was one other thing about that lamp.

It was still lit!

Jake called Cleo the biggest liar he had ever heard.

Cleo acquiesced, but made a counter offer. "Jake, knock two hundred pounds off your sailfish ... I'll blow out my lamp."

Michael Toia

Frog Tongues

We were contractors, often spending a week or so per job at the Space Coast. There was a superb, cozy restaurant riverside at the Eau Gallie causeway, one of our favorite watering holes. Ambiance was wonderful. Food was good. Prices were moderate. All in all, it was always worth the visit.

Work proceeded throughout the day and into the early evening, as we prepared for a test. Those prep sessions were always interesting, intense, and engaging, of the type that caused one to lose track of the passage of time. The work was psychologically very rewarding. We chipped away, hour after hour, and were brought back to the clock by rumblings in the stomach area. "Hey! I'm running on empty down here. Where the heck is food?" And when the stomach spoke, it was time to break away and satisfy it.

A particularly fine evening found me at that juncture. Preparations for the test were well along, and the remainder could wait for, and profit from, a good night's rest. So off I went, this time solo, to seek out a restaurant before retiring to my motel room. Eau Gallie came to mind.

It was after nine P.M. when I arrived riverside and parked the car. Shortly I was inside, and pleasantly seated at a small table well off the main floor area, with a nice view of the river.

Not a wine connoisseur, I confess that alcoholic drinks never appealed to me. The wife and I will occasionally have a glass on our anniversary. Otherwise the wine list is set aside. The menu, however, is quite another thing. It collaborated with hunger to suggest many possible epicurean delights. What to order? What to order? I continued my study, for thereupon were many interesting offerings, and a most unusual one sprang forth from the page ... Linguini with Frogs' Legs.

Well! It's not often that one finds frogs' legs on the menu, and over the years, my first foray into that delicacy, as an attempt at a joke, led to a bit of a passion. They curry my favor, as I have grown rather fond of that fare. They always remind me of a Simpson's program episode themed against The Exodus with the following exchange:

Pharo (dining): "Ummm ... these frogs' legs are delicious!"

Moses: "It's a plague, you idiot!"

When the waiter approached to take my order, so it was ... the Linguini and Frogs' Legs.

The ambiance and comfort, enhanced by the view of the river, were accepted with appreciation. Relaxation and anticipation of a good meal made the short wait most pleasant. In a most reasonable time my order arrived, and the preparation was excellent – green spinach linguini noodles, plump frogs' legs in a delicious tomato-based, thick sauce, all served with a light sprinkling of herbs that set off the flavor of the dish, and wonderful garlic toast. I began. The legs were prepared to perfection, the linguini likewise, and the sauce just exquisite.

As I continued, the small leg bones began to pile up on the edge of my plate. By and by, a group of three young couples with an infant or two was seated at a larger table toward the center of the restaurant, adjoining mine. They chatted. Their infants were very well behaved, did not cry or carry on, and I applaud them for that. They studied the menu. They spoke in normal tones, but could not help from being overheard at my table.

A young mother seated closest to me, facing their table, seemed to grimace and shiver a bit. "Frogs' legs! Oh, no! How could anyone eat such things?" The others quietly and politely 'shushed'

Michael Toia

her, informing her of my meal and presence. I continued, not wanting to enter their conversation, and particularly not wanting to add to the mental anguish already being expressed

The young lady then turned about, viewed myself and my table, shuddered noticeably, and turned back to face her friends. I avoided eye contact, again not wanting in any way to add to the discomfort she already expressed about that particular menu entrée, and continued dining.

She and her company talked a bit more. Then she turned again toward me. It was obvious she wished to make eye contact, and perhaps conversation. I engaged into both.

She said, "Excuse me, sir; may I ask? Is that the frogs' legs entree?"

I answered pleasantly in the affirmative. She turned back toward her company. I picked up a single, fairly long strand of green linguini noodle, dangling it from my fork. At that precise time she turned again, and asked, "And what is that?"

I was caught completely off-guard, did not know exactly what to say, or how to say it. I could have been rude and told her just to buzz off and stop bothering me. But she and her group were so pleasant, I did not want to be insulting, do or say anything that might place an additional flaw in their otherwise evening out with friends. I tried to be as cordial as I could.

I looked at that green, flat, linguini noodle, a bit over an eighth of an inch wide, doubled over a tine of my fork, its two ends hanging vertically about five inches, just above the plate, flecks of that thick, red sauce clinging to it patch-wise over its length. And what I said … To this day, I am apologetic and remorseful about those awful two words. I meant only to be as pleasant as possible, and not to spoil her evening any more than my choice of entree had. Looking again at my fork, the green linguini, the red specks of thick sauce, I said, with absolutely no rehearsal, no malice of forethought, what just popped into my mind at the moment … "The tongues."

It was probably the worst possible thing that could have been said. She gulped, placed her hand over her mouth, sprang from her chair, and ran … I presume to the ladies' room.

The group at her table said nothing to me. I simply realized what had happened, looked as apologetic as I could, and broke eye contact with all of them. I finished my meal shortly after and departed. I wanted to apologize to the young lady, but did not see her again. Nevertheless, I am to this day sorry for being the cause of her distress on an otherwise pleasant evening.

If you are she, please forgive me, so I may go to my grave in peace.

Michael Toia

Lottery

Florida is an interesting state, and its Space Coast draws many visitors, some of it the contractor base catering to the industry there. Florida also runs a lottery, as do many states and, at one time, there had been a spell of several months with no payout. The lottery jackpot grew and grew, and got to be quite an attractive prize for some lucky soul.

A mild frenzy set in. People were rushing about, buying lottery tickets. Even several of my contractor colleagues got into the act, taking the chance that they might be the lucky one. After all, the cost of the ticket was a constant, but the potential payoff, a variable, had increased rather enormously.

The logic goes along these lines. For a dollar invested in a ticket, at a half million dollar jackpot, and a million to one odds of winning, you will, in the long run, win 50 cents on the dollar. You will be a long-term loser.

But if the odds remain at a million to one, and the ticket price remains the same, a 100 million dollar jackpot will return 100 dollars per dollar spent. You will be a long-term winner! So play, already. And that type of logic was published in the newspapers, magazines, billboards, on the radio talk shows, and on, and on, and on ... Well, the possibility of winning 100 to one, or a hundred bucks per buck invested, can be whipped up further. Suppose you buy a thousand dollars worth of lottery tickets? You will, in the long run, win 100 thousand dollars.

Now let's return to reality. Merritt Island is separated from the west bank of the Indian River by the river itself. Homes on the west side of the island face the west bank, and thereupon was a grocery store, just across the river from those homes, and it sold lottery tickets. It was by far the closest outlet where a resident at that part of the island could buy a ticket. So one hopeful chap thought deeply on the matter, and while there was yet time before the day's drawing, went to his little boat dock.

He hopped into a small, aluminum 'duck boat,' fired up its outboard and went across the river to buy a ticket ... or, perhaps, many tickets. And, by golly, he made the news!

It seems that the odds of hitting the jackpot are far less than the odds of being hit by lightning. Both are rather small, one much smaller than the other. But this chap beat those odds.

He did not win the lottery. On the return trip he was, however, struck by lightning ... so the morning paper claimed. It also claimed he did survive, and was in the hospital.

Michael Toia

Microwave Eggs

The microwave oven was born of radar research in World War II. Technicians found that, if they stood close to a powerful radar antenna, they felt a warming sensation. In fact, their whole body warmed, as it absorbed the microwave power. This effect is employed by diathermy machines for medical treatment. In addition, they found, sometimes by accident, that the then-prevalent photo flash bulbs would go off near these antennas, and steel wool would ignite. It wasn't long before an enterprising individual thought of using that effect to cook food.

After the war the "Radar Range" was introduced. It was basically an oven, a metal box, which at microwave frequencies is called a "resonant cavity." A powerful radar magnetron tube shot its microwave power into the cavity. Food inside would then heat and cook, and this is the principle by which the modern microwave oven works.

When the first such ovens were introduced into the market, there was concern that the microwaves they generated might leak out and cause interference to radar or radio devices, and that if there were sufficient leakage, the cook himself might be injured. The former concern fell to the Federal Communications Commission, or FCC; the latter to the Bureau of Radiological Health. I spent several years as an FCC engineer and heard this story from the ones who evaluated the first microwave ovens.

An oven was submitted to the FCC laboratory for tests. It needed something to cook. Early on, a decision was made to put a container of water inside. The amount of water was related to the oven's power rating.

Ed was the engineer running the test. He was a pro-technology fellow, as are nearly all engineers. He saw a future for this device.

It happened that Ed lived on a small farm, and kept chickens. So one morning he brought an egg to the lab. He tried microwaving the egg, in its shell. My boss and mentor Milt, the lab chief, told me the story initially, and concluded, "... with the result that the egg did detonate, thereby vulcanizing its contents to the innards of the oven." He had quite a delightful mannerism with words, and I had a hearty laugh about the tale. Later Ed, a personal friend, confided that the description was certainly true, and it took him a week to clean all the egg from the oven's inside.

Ed did not give up. He tried microwaving an egg, sunny-side up on a Pyrex plate. Milt's description was, "... the yolk thereof did detonate, with much the same result as previously." Another hearty laugh, and again Ed confirmed the truth.

Came the time the FCC was revising technical standards for microwave ovens. We convened a joint industry-government committee to study the matter and advise on consequences and technical parameters of the change. I chaired the committee.

As the first session was gathering, I opened with an icebreaker, detailing Ed's experience. Everyone had a good laugh ... except for one attendee, Gene. He had a rather sober story to relate, following mine.

Gene's company was an early one offering microwave ovens for sale to the public. A young couple were married, and received one as a wedding present. After the reception and acceptance of presents, they departed on honeymoon.

On their return, the new bride dutifully sent 'thank you' notes acknowledging the many gifts. The microwave oven intrigued her.

At a morning breakfast, she placed an egg in an egg cup, set the assembly inside, and turned the oven ON. "Oh, no!" I said. "It exploded, making a mess out of the oven!"

Gene said, "Not yet. It cooked. She removed it from the oven, carried it proudly to her new hubby and, wanting to please and impress him, plunked it down in front of him with a flourish.

"THEN it exploded! He was covered with scalding hot egg. He thought she was trying to assassinate him. He sued for annulment.

"She was reduced to tears. She wanted only to please him. She was distraught that he would think so horribly of one who loved him so.

"They went to court. By and by the micro-waved "exploding egg" phenomenon was introduced, and accepted as a fault. The wife was exonerated. The couple reconciled. My company was sued. We settled out of court for a sizeable award.

"THAT's why we now warn others not to microwave an egg, except for poaching in a special dish, or in scrambled form."

Everyone had a good laugh, except Gene, and we all made note of the microwave egg situation. The wise are cautioned. Fools will, of course, try microwaving whole eggs. They will repeat Ed's experience. We engineers try to make our products foolproof, but nothing is ... for fools are so ingenious.

Near Death

The year was 1972. A new regional office was being established. Its keynote feature computer would be honed to the local needs, and hold a large database tracking daily conduct of business. Such endeavors do not happen overnight. Much planning went into the project before an advanced cadre departed from corporate headquarters. I was in that cadre.

Business included a lot of engineering analysis, to be part of the new computer's function. Our engineering branch had continual telephone contact with headquarters, where the brunt of computer programming was being done.

An admin branch gathered information about the region and built a database, supporting both administrative and analytic functions. The ops branch operated the new computer, and tended it through its installation and build up "from scratch." The fledgling machine was exercised to test the algorithms produced by corporate computer analysts. It had a handful of separable functions: common administrative work, human resources, payroll, building the database, and testing the engineering programs that riffled through that database. Each function demanded its share of computer time. The last one was my responsibility.

Engineering programs were a small set of computer runs that, as it happened, took about ten minutes on the average. We did this for several months. In that day, the laptop and PC were yet a gleam in their inventors' eyes. The computer, affectionately but with a touch of irreverence called "glitchie kludgie," occupied its own room, sat on a raised floor of 2' x 2' heavy metal tiles, required its own air conditioning system, and was quite large by year 2012 cell phone or iPad standards. Glitchie possessed a brain size about that of half a flea, running at speeds rivaling that of a slow walk.

The intermixed demands on glitchie required its operators to schedule various 'jobs' and avoid conflicts. Database building and engineering analysis could not be run simultaneously. The former was adding to and correcting the database, while the latter would consult that base for an updated estimate of the region's structure in a 'snapshot' mode. To do so, it had to 'open' the database, read it, and then 'close' it.

The ubiquitous PCs forty years later had an operating system – a common one being MS Windows – that took care of one important function, such as denial of permission to modify a document file that is 'open' and being written to by another program. The file must be closed, then reopened by another program wanting to write to it, else the system loses the ability to track the "breadcrumbs" trail of all the tiny pieces called sectors that, chained together, are the entire file. Garbage results when this chaining sequence is lost.

Operating systems then had flaws in file management. Since glitchie initially ran only one program at a time, the need of such management had not appeared, but was about to. The computer gurus of the day were bright young lassies and laddies. They developed the concept of "multitasking." If a given job used but a fraction of a computer's resources, why not run two or more simultaneously? What a great idea! And so, they created an operating system that would do just that. Our upgraded system could run four jobs simultaneously!

Alas, the operating system would not check for conflicting crisscrossing of those breadcrumbs when more than one program would use the same data file. Errors and crashes that came about as a result led to the development of better file management procedures for next generation computers

Engineering runs would be prepared and stacked up as groups of "punched cards," the input system of the day. When glitchie was not in use by other functions, and according to a "pecking order" of job importance, engineering would be run, one at a time, at about ten minutes each.

Staff members from corporate were regular visitors. They worked with us days. At night they retired to a cocktail lounge to while away their time away from home. Some of our local staff felt it necessary to spend their evenings that way. Some did not; I was one of the nots. And that set the stage for a near-homicide.

We knew that engineering jobs had to be run in a specified sequence. An order – my order – to that effect had been posted in the computer room, on the operators' special instructions board. The cocktail crowd gave our operations a lot of thought. The posted order notwithstanding, they decided that multitasking four engineering jobs simultaneously could speed things considerably. The guidance of several martinis deemed this an excellent plan. It was adopted about 9 P.M. one fateful evening at the standard watering hole.

Results were a disaster: run after run 'crashed' and failed to complete properly. Two months of growing frustration and deep agony resulted. Test throughput fell to practically zero. Corporate programmers were baffled. Things that earlier ran flawlessly now failed. Stacks of that large 'z-fold' 132-column computer paper, outputs of failed runs, began piling up in my office. We were about at wit's end. Many a night's sleep was lost over the matter.

Finally my good friend and programmer at corporate, studying the copious "core dumps" whereby glitchie cursed at us in gobs of hex, [1] noticed an oddity: the program runs that failed were running concurrently, each trying to access and modify the same files in the

---

[1] Hexadecimal numbers. Computers then and now deal in bit strings of 1s and 0s, and a shortcut way of presenting a long string of these is to combine four at a time into a single character from a set of sixteen, from 0 through 9, and A through F. An example: 36 bits can be expressed as 7AF30091C. So it was and is.

database. Hence glitchie lost track of those file breadcrumb trails: both runs were competing to rearrange the crumbs, losing the file structure continuities.

AHA! Problem found. So why was I not diligent and keeping track of the operators so they did not multi-task engineering jobs? Why, indeed? Good question. I left my office and walked to the computer room, through the door and up the ramp, to the operators' special instructions board. And, thereupon was that special order, stating engineering runs were to be submitted consecutively and never concurrently.

With the order pointed out, the computer operator on duty was questioned and asked why the runs were, in fact, run concurrently. He said his boss, chief of computer ops, had issued the instruction some time ago. We summoned his chief by the intercom. He arrived. We discussed the matter. Chief of ops said the resident systems analyst, Doug, had issued the order, which ops had even questioned in light of the special order.

As luck would have it, in strolled the very culprit. I approached Doug, asked what the devil was going on, and why the order was being violated. Then the cocktail hour story was revealed, of how corporate and he had discussed speeding up computer ops, and how the concurrent-running instruction came about.

By this time, I had become quite visibly disturbed. My entire body began venting frustration, with an angered statement that the matter had been crashing engineering runs for a full two months, causing no end of anguish. My face likely showed the stress, as Doug began backing away, toward the wall, to no net gain. We stayed together as if conjoined, my exposition of frustration, ruined runs, lack of sleep, and so forth taking on the tone of a tirade. He backed against a large window, four floors above the parking lot.

I then came to realize that my left arm was cocked and its fist clenched, ready to remove his head. Fortunately sufficient presence of mind found the means to stop, and then slowly *and painfully* lower the arm. I turned toward the door, stomped down the ramp and into the main office bullpen area, pulling the door smartly closed behind me ... perhaps too smartly. The doorknob shot off its spindle and began noisily clinking about twenty feet across the floor. This offered little comfort, but rather further annoyance.

The corridor to my office was about a hundred feet across the bullpen. I stomped and snorted across. The only noise was that wayward doorknob, and my snorting and stomping. The staff's work, noise, chatter, and breathing came to a complete halt for the moment, until a few moments following my bull-like charge to my room and the hundreds of stacks of that z-fold computer paper in large piles all about.

I picked up one stack, held it a moment, and then set it down smartly ... very smartly ... on my large worktable. The table was not up to the force of my action, as it broke in two, spilling its contents onto the floor. This further infuriated me: gainful work could not continue that afternoon. It was 2 P.M.

I strolled back down the hall at a good clip, turned the corner, left the office area, and summoned the elevator. After an interminable wait of five seconds, I abandoned the quest and stomped down the stairwell. My wife was at school some twenty miles away, and we were to meet about 6:30 P.M. Charging on to the metro stop, then waiting for the train, revealed a pay phone on the platform. Yes, this was well before cell phones. Call Corporate, I thought, tell them the problem has been discovered. A dime found its assisted way from a pocket to the phone box. It was 1972, after all.

No dial tone! And ... the thing would not return the dime. More frustration! Would nothing go right that day? I gave the handset a light tug, and its armored cord came completely out of the phone box. Stunned, standing there a few seconds, examining the phone and its now-detached handset, the latter firmly in my grip, I hurled the thing from the platform down onto the track area. It hit a rail and literally exploded into shards, hundreds of them. And, still, the train had not arrived. Deciding that, to cool off, I would walk the mile from that platform to the next, the action was begun, and completed before the scheduled train's arrival.

When at last it did, I boarded, rode downtown, transferred trains, and rode to the university. A walk of about four blocks put me at the building to meet my wife, in the computer lab – in those days, a bank of keypunch machines.

Entering therein, I looked about, saw my gorgeous bride, and finally felt some small relief. As I strolled up behind her and approached amid the rattling and clanking din of all those machines, she suddenly stopped typing, turned about, saw me, and said, "My God! What happened?"

I said, "What?"

She stopped her work immediately, picked up her cards and coding sheets, rose, and said, "You should see your face! Let's go … what happened?"

It was 4:30 P.M.

We left together, walked over to a little restaurant, had a light supper before our evening classes, and she, being the ever devoted spouse, heard me out, listened to my every word, and placated me back to normal.

I thought that my episode would lead to a firing. It happened on Tuesday. With stiffened resolve, I returned to work the next morning, completed the work week by cleaning up the office and seeing to it that the engineering runs were being done properly. It was not until Friday morning my boss finally approached the office, peered in the door, and said, "I hear there was some sort of altercation Tuesday?"

I briskly said, "Yup!" And he left.

Not long after, I was actually promoted to corporate, brought back to where I had been, having participated for three years in bringing the new office on line. And few people now countermand my orders without discussion and seeking approval first.

Justifiable Abacuscide

January, 1972. We were transferred to Illinois. The move had been planned. We worked out our income tax filings for Federal and our previous State, and kept them in a briefcase, as there was to be a change of address. Dutifully we filed both returns on time, after entering our new Illinois address. We were expecting a refund check.

Illinois became a pleasant place once May arrived and the trees finally began to leaf out. The winter, though, was a mite cold. We had come from South of the Mason-Dixon Line. Biking, sailing, and canoeing – our three interests – became very pleasant, indeed. That, and exploration of our new surroundings was quite enjoyable.

About July the news contained a story about tax cheats. Many people filed a Federal return giving an Illinois address, but failed to file an Illinois return. Illinois said they were going to crack down on these deadbeats.

Ahhhhh … perhaps you now smell the plot of this story?

Yes, a few months later, we received a mailing from Illinois Department of Revenue. It said we gave an Illinois address on our Federal return, but did not file an Illinois return for the previous year. An examination of our Federal return indicated that we owed Illinois so and so much income tax, plus interest, plus penalty for not filing.

A quite understandable mistake. We prepared a short letter in response, stating that we moved to Illinois in January, did not live in Illinois at any time the previous year, so were not required to file an Illinois return, nor pay income tax to the state. Both my wife and I signed the letter, which was then consigned to the US Post Office.

Not long after we received a reply. To our surprise, it indicated that we were still deeply in arrears, the interest was increased, and more penalties were being assessed. We were young and unlearned at the time. The proper response to such a letter is not to the department of revenue, but to your elected State and Federal Representatives. To the department you are but a peon, and pee on you they do. But to a state or US representative, you are a voter. The peeing order reverses.

Uneducated in that fact, we answered the second letter, explaining once again the situation, and included a copy of our settlement sheets on sale of our former residence and purchase of our Illinois residence, with dates highlighted.

Alas, this was to no avail. In another few weeks, we received another epistle from the department, saying they were to garnish my wages, send the Sheriff out to bring me before their judge, read me my rights, and exact still more penalty. This, of course, caused our anguish to deepen considerably.

After an initial gut-wrenching, my anger rose to a new height. At the time I worked with a few systems analysts, one a rather retro individual whose talents and expertise were a decade behind the present. I could now see his counterpart at the department who concocted the computer program, which searched the federal database, but forgot that about five percent of the population move each year. Idiots of this variety cause grief to many of us and ought to be banned from the kingdom, or at the very minimum neutered and put aside, rendered thereby incapable of further corruption of the nation's gene pool, and prevented from interfacing with the general public. And if this harsh comment seems offensive, YOU are the likely the one I am addressing. Shame! Go sit in the corner somewhere for a hundred years.

Michael Toia

Now armed with flowing adrenalin, I began preparing a rather nice letter response to the department, which indicated that I knew computers, worked with them, and knew Springfield, the State capital, and just where the computer sat, which was the cause of my grief. The letter further instructed that I had both the knowledge and the wherewithal to put that computer to the task of totally and irretrievably scrambling its entire database, but would restrain myself should the department read my earlier letters and understand that a bonehead computer systems analyst was loose in their midst.

It also instructed that, on receipt of their next threatening letter, I would put my plan to action, destroy their database, and likely maim the responsible systems analyst. If prosecuted for these actions, I would claim "criminal mental anguish and justifiable abacuscide – the murder of a calculating machine." This, having been writ, sought my signature, which was provided thereupon.

This frightened my wife. She refused to sign. No matter … the letter leaped into the closest mailbox.

I expected to hear from the department one way or another. The year was 1972. It is now 2012. Word has yet to be received. Neither demanded taxes, nor interest, nor penalties have been paid.

Are you listening, Illinois?

There is a sequel to this story. Three years after the Illinois transfer, corporate brought me back to my original location. We sold our residence. The purchaser sought unusual financing, as he was a member of the Polish Roman Catholic Union … honestly, as well as I can recall. The Union offered its members loans at lower interest than the prevailing rate.

We moved. We waited. We lived in an efficiency unit at a motel for several months. The buyer still did not obtain his financing. Someone at the Union apparently fouled up his paperwork. But at long, long last the sale completed, and we bought a house in our new location. We endured that motel for 108 days.

Several months following, a large post card arrived from the sheriff's office at our old Illinois location. It indicated that the taxes on our previous home had not been paid, and were they not, the property would be put up for sheriff's sale for unpaid taxes at 8 A.M. Central Time, April 2.

The card asked what course of action we preferred. It had five lines with little boxes at the beginning of each, asked us to check a box, and return the form. The choices were:

☐ Taxes in full plus interest are being paid by return mail.

☐ Half the taxes are being paid and I will call to arrange final payment.

☐ I will call to make arrangements to pay the due taxes.

☐ I request a court hearing on the matter.

☐ Other _____

The line following 'other' was about an inch long. I checked its box. On it I printed, legibly but in small font:

PROCEED WITH SALE.

The returned postcard apparently satisfied and flushed their computer of our name. We have yet to hear to the contrary.

Curious, though, what the scene was at eight in the morning, the following April 2, on my former front lawn? Ahhh, well ...some things are better left to the imagination.

Ex-Post Fascist

Our Maryland home, in an unincorporated part of Howard County to the East of a small town, ZIP Code 21029, was serviced by its post office. That is how we received our mail ... until ... One day our rural mail box was stuffed. There were seven ... yes, seven ... Sears catalogs therein, each with a variant spelling of our surname, none quite correct. In those pre-Internet days, customers who bought a good deal from Sears received an annual catalog in the mail.

We called Sears and said we needed but one and also gave them the proper spelling of our surname. But that must have fallen into the crack, as shortly thereafter we received a bill for our monthly purchases, made out to one of the seven misspellings of our name. We reasoned that we wanted our name to receive credit for prompt and proper payment, so sent the bill back to Sears, unpaid, with a letter stating that, by some weird coincidence, the billed party had purchased exactly the same items we had purchased, yet we did not receive a bill.

We received a correctly-spelled bill about three days later, and promptly paid same.

But I run off on a tangent to the main point. Our large mailbox sat on a post down at the lane. Neighborhood rascals liked to come through and detonate some small bomb in the box, run it down with their pickup truck, or otherwise destroy it. I finally, tired of replacement, took a post office box near my office in Columbia, MD, ZIP 21044.

I visited the Department of Motor Vehicles – DMV – to change our address. They said they could not accept a Post Office Box number as an official address, and needed the exact street address. I told them I was in the same house, so they said to do nothing.

Now the nearby new city of Columbia was expanding, and expand they did – they engulfed our neighborhood and home, one of many old, pre-Columbian artifacts. The postmaster at Columbia, ZIP 21045, sent us a note that we had one year to notify all our correspondents of the address change, and thereafter his office would no longer forward mail with the old ZIP code. We did so with each correspondence that we answered.

Our insurance company sent us a renewal notice. The one-year forwarding period had expired. The notice was not delivered, but was returned. The insurance company then sent a notice by registered mail. *It* was not delivered, whereupon the insurance company assumed that we had simply changed insurers, and notified the DMV that they no longer were our carriers.

The DMV checked their records. We were uninsured. They mailed us a notice requiring proof of insurance, again beyond the one year forwarding limit. It was never delivered.

On a cold, drizzly February Monday evening I returned home about 6 P.M. My wife was due in about a half hour. On our doorknob a rolled paper attached with a rubber band, from the DMV, announced that both our drivers' licenses and auto registrations would be canceled on the indicated date – the previous Friday!

What! I had no idea what had happened, but by now was rather more educated, so, though trembling considerably, called the local office of my US representative. A young lady answered. I haltingly explained the evening's course of actions and my mystification about it. She asked that I drive to their office immediately, saying not to worry about a canceled license, but to come without delay. I did so. She was puzzled as well, but took a report. She said she would call the head of the DMV about 2 A.M.

"2 A.M.?" I asked.

"Yes. He will not be busy, will be home, will take my call, and have the matter on his mind when he reaches his office later in the morning."

So that's how it works! Interesting. And I presume she did just that. The next day she called me, and gave me the full explanation, which I describe below.

The DMV tried to reach us by mail, but could not, so sent the sheriff to deliver the notice in person. She found that the postmaster was the 'gum' in the machinery. She had contacted my insurance company, and found a resolution: If I agreed to pay the premium that had been due, my insurer would tell DMV there had been a small error, DMV would accept the explanation, and our licenses and registration would be reinstated as if nothing had happened.

We accepted this offer and paid the premium.

I was then asked to visit my US representative's office on The Hill to tell my story. Several others and I did so.

One chap told an interesting story. He was the county clerk of elections, said that historically the county seat was a thriving community when one Benjamin Franklin thought the new country needed a post office service. He appeared as if a contemporary of Franklin, a charming man my senior by several decades.

His story: The county sends absentee ballots to service members and others not living at home. They have no expiration date! And, at the last election, it came to light that, because of the ZIP code change, over four thousand were not forwarded by the post office in time to be counted. People were being denied their right to vote.

The several of us departed the hill. I returned to my office about noon. Our maintenance man made the daily mail run after lunch, returned, and announced, "You'll never guess what happened at the post office!"

The staff was naturally piqued. He continued: "A black limo with government plates drove into the parking lot. Four suits [2] got out and came into the post office, right to the front of the line. The clerk said they had to wait their turn. They showed some kind of identification, said they did not. They asked to see the postmaster. The clerk got him. They had a short discussion and four suits left, got into the limo that then drove off. One of the leaving suits was the now-ex postmaster!"

And that's the story of ZIP 21045's fascist ex-postmaster and his replacement. Lightning sometimes strikes its intended target, and this was a goood hit. Waaay to go, God! I am deeply, deeply impressed!

---

[2] Slang for a very important-looking person wearing a business suit.

Spooky

Cheryl had just graduated from high school and answered an ad seeking a job. She became a computer operator-trainee in our office. She was young, very pleasant, attractive, and a really good worker. Cheryl worked the day shift where the majority of operations occurred, strong mentoring was available, and where personal safety during commute time might be best.

The computer, or glitchie as we called it, performed a variety of tasks. One was a set of engineering test jobs under my command. These all had the same characteristic structure, a grab of bunches of data from glitchie's data storage units, followed by several seconds of deep thought and number crunching, repeating cyclically about eight times a minute for ten minutes.

Now there is a small effect known as electromagnetic interference, or EMI, a fancy techno-geek term meaning man-made static. You have likely heard EMI. Tune a transistor radio to the AM band, about to the middle of the dial somewhere between stations, and then bring it close to your computer monitor or TV set. A lot of noisy static should be heard.

Glitchie was no exception. I had a small radio in my office, about two hundred feet from the computer room, and could hear a light static in the pleasant music from my favorite station. It dawned on me that the static was, in fact, due to glitchie's thought processes.

Every now and then the static would be a general background 'hash' for a few seconds, then a more musical pulsing noise for a few seconds. Subconsciously, I came to recognize this as one of my engineering jobs that glitchie was running. I'd continue my normal work for some seven minutes, then yawn, stretch, and start toward glitchie's room.

Through the door and up the ramp I would stroll, behind the operator's position, and look at the monitor screen. In less than a minute my run would complete and be assigned to the printer. I'd walk to the printer, wait the minute or so for it to finish, tear the stack of paper from it, and depart. This became a routine, retrieving about six or so runs a day.

Several months later Len, the chief of computer ops, sat in my office. Colleagues and also personal friends, we discussed how things were going. He asked if I had seen Cheryl recently.

I mused, "No, come to think of it. Did she quit? I thought you were rather pleased with her work. You didn't fire her, did you?"

"No," he said, "she works night shift. She requested night shift. She is afraid of you."

"What!" I exclaimed. "Good grief, what did I do? I'm shocked to hear that."

"You spooked her." He continued. "Time and again she would submit one of your runs. She saw it start on her monitor. In nine minutes you would appear behind her, look over her shoulder, see the monitor, watch your job finish, walk to the printer, take your output and leave. She is convinced you are some sort of devil or deity, some sort of spirit, and she is genuinely frightened about it."

Len continued. "You and I are co-workers, personal friends. Cheryl may fear you, but not me. I want to know how you do that."

I was quite taken aback. But after just a minute of further chatter, my radio began its familiar cadence. I said, "Listen to the music a bit. Notice anything unusual?"

Len listened. He said, "What's that rhythmic noise in the background?" I explained. We waited seven minutes, then strolled to his computer room. He saw my run complete, we took the printer output, and returned to my office. I said, "Voila."

Len said, "I knew there was a logical explanation. I know you well. I know you're not a spook, and expected you engineers had not bugged my computer." We had a good laugh about it.

Len later explained the whole thing to Cheryl. She did not buy it. And to my disappointment, I never saw her again, and am truly sorry I had spooked her.

If you are Cheryl, please forgive me. I am about as spooky as a cup of water, and despite conjecture to the contrary, I'm just an ordinary engineer and manager with no special paranormal powers at all. More's the pity, though … I could use them.

The Simulator

My sweet spouse, reared in a household devoid of firearms, married into a family and a society a scant ten miles distant, where every household had at least one for each and every male resident. These were means for provision of food, well-utilized hunting implements. At first shocked and frightened as she accidentally came across my trusty rifle, a .22 Winchester model 60A, she acclimatized to the matter rather nicely.

An uncle, an auxiliary policeman, lived close by my hometown. On a visit as newlyweds we found, or rather heard, uncle and a few others out behind the house practicing a bit with his police revolver. It was a trusty Smith and Wesson .38 Special. Now, neither Joyce nor I had fired a handgun, but uncle was quite gracious, and showed us how to handle the weapon. We were both coached through taking a few shots of our own. I instinctively recalled the four safety rules of firearms, took a shot or two at targets a few tens of feet distant, and got my first feel of handgun use.

Joyce's previous home life had not drilled that four-rule basic training into her. Uncle prepared the pistol for firing, gave her proper instruction, pointed her downrange and placed the gun in her hand. He coached her into an aim and a trigger pull. The weapon did its thing, with its characteristic resounding BOOM and recoil. This, being her first firing, was an entirely new experience. She turned about, uttered an excited, "Wow!" and held the gun, now pointing not downrange but more or less at the few of us behind her. Uncle immediately took Joyce's gun hand wrist firmly and pushed it skyward, then slowly and carefully extracted the gun from her hand, coaching her through the process and admonishing here in unquestionable, yet polite, terms about control of the weapon and where it is pointing. There was no shooting accident.

My sweets became accustomed to having a gun in the house. We would occasionally take the Winchester to a worked-out quarry and 'plink' at small targets we set up for the purpose. A .22 rifle has practically no recoil, no 'kick,' just a pleasant POP instead of a BOOM, and is a nice way of learning to enjoy target shooting.

Many years later, we relocated and moved to a small farm in a backwater county of Florida. I operated a small business in its barn and in a tiny shop in the nearby town. It was, indeed, a rural setting; the county population fewer than fifteen thousand souls, more or less. Cattle ranching, agriculture, and tree farming were the primary activities.

We discovered to our chagrin that the farm housed quite a population of reptiles, primarily snakes, some poisonous, some not. Nonetheless, we were wary of the lot and had not the knowledge to tell one from the other. The Winchester 60A was not up to the task of reptile defense. Advice sought from the locals instructed that we obtain and carry a .38 revolver, the first two chambers loaded with birdshot to engage the moccasins crawling about, and three after that with hollow point to engage rabid raccoons. Its sixth and final chamber was to be left empty as a standard safety procedure.

Unfortunately, the price of such a tool was rather high. We acquired instead a .410 shotgun at the local Western Auto store. It was up to the task, and took on control of the creepy-crawler community. As memory serves, about a half dozen snakes per week were thus dispatched the entire three years of our living there. Our 'arsenal,' so to speak, now was the two, the .22 rifle and the shotgun.

There were other noxious critters about – a two-legged variety – and through their agency, we were relieved of ownership of two

Michael Toia

small boats, a number of tools from the barn, and a few thousand dollars of inventory from our in-town shop. We decided to leave and return to a more civilized, less crime-ridden lifestyle. Shortly after, one Hinckley took a shot at President Reagan, and another at Jim Brady, wounding both but killing neither. This led to the Brady 'one handgun a month' bill that became law.

Joyce, now knowing the importance of firearms in daily life as a tool toward existence and defense, presented me with a Smith and Wesson .38 Special pistol, the very same model as we had fired under uncle's tutorage so many years previous, and my first handgun. Our arsenal grew slightly.

Now, we were and remain, not 'gun nuts,' but realize the need for such as tools of defense, dependent on one's environment. We also realize that the proper use of tools requires proper training and reasonable practice sessions. My sweets came across a firm that provides both on a simulated, indoor handgun range. The pistols are real, but do not fire bullets. They are equipped with laser sights and are 'fired' at a target projected on a life-sized movie screen. A computer system locates the laser's spot on the screen and projects appropriate indication of the shot, sometimes an exaggerated hole in an image of a target, sometimes a more dramatic effect. An audio system plays back the sound of gunfire. The simulation is quite real, absent only the smell of burnt gunpowder and recoil of the pistol.

That year my birthday present was an evening's session on the simulator. It was wonderful.

After an initial period of instruction through how to hold and operate the pistol and the four safety rules, the simulation led to sighting, test firing, how to improve one's stance and gun control, and how to improve one's accuracy and precision. The latter is a measure of the diameter of a circle that is just large enough to contain a small group of shots; the former, the distance between the center of that circle and the center of the target. One might achieve high precision with low accuracy or the opposite. Practice seeks to improve both simultaneously.

We stood there, side by side, she on my right and I to the left. As the session proceeded, more and more interesting target sets were presented, none being human, all static, inanimate scenes. And it came to pass ... the scene became black. We were in a dimly lit room, simulating outdoors. Narration from the system's sound track announced, "Shooter on the right! A farm scene will appear, five fence posts, a target atop each. Engage targets, left to right."

The scene appeared. There stood the wooden fence image, its five posts, and a watermelon atop each. Joyce took aim, fired, and the leftmost image exploded into flying bits of simulated watermelon in all directions, exaggeratingly dramatic. She fired again, thrice, four times, and five. Each time the appropriate watermelon did the same. She had acquired skill, precision, and accuracy sufficient to the task, and dispatched the five targets.

The scene again faded to black. Her score was projected on the screen for a wee bit, then it, too, faded. Narration continued. "Shooter on the left! Same scenario. Engage targets left to right." I stood in eager anticipation, knowing that I had to come close to her performance, drooled a bit, held my pistol at the ready, anticipating, anticipating ...

The scene appeared. There was the fence, the background farm scene, absent any accidental targets such as animals, people, machinery or anything that could, by accident, be killed or destroyed; and on the posts appeared my five targets ... beer cans!

Now, wait a minute, I thought. Where are the watermelons? These things are a good deal smaller, more difficult targets. This was, after all, *my* birthday present! Had Joyce colluded with the simulator operator to play this trick on me? And then, she gave herself away. Though the room was dimly lit, I heard her sweet, pleasant voice give out with a bit of an involuntary giggle.

I was challenged!

Perhaps I should have considered divorce at that time. This was a mean trick. But divorce was as far from my mind as could be. I enjoyed the prank fully, for I have learned to love that woman from the bottom of my heart and innermost part of my soul, though my own bit of chuckling over the matter did have a negative effect on my accuracy and precision. But, with careful aim, the five targets were dispatched, one shot each, and I saved face.

Misogyny? Baloney! You feminists are ridiculous! Women always get the upper hand.

Blue Streak

The Army at peace prepares for war. It rests in posts, camps, and stations. Its troops are given unusually meaningless tasks. "Dig a hole! Fill it in! Dig another hole!" This is akin to an athlete's calisthenics – exercises to get and keep in shape until actual performance is required.

Field maneuvers are a more extensive and intricate form of exercise than hole digging. Generals of higher commands make plans, and selected Army units are divided into two – 'Red' forces, 'Blue' forces. A small additional grouping is established as 'Umpire' forces. The Red and Blue conduct mock attacks against each other, and the umpires review the action, scoring each side, ultimately choosing a winner in the war game. The aftermath is studied, yielding its 'lessons learned' that help future planning, be it mock battle or real.

We were assigned to a fort, troops living in barracks, doing daily exercises on the thousands of acres, usually returning to home barracks in the evenings, sometimes bunking down outdoors during more extensive training incidents. We trained on maintenance and usage of our equipment, and kept everything in a high state of readiness should the nation call on us for real. It was October, 1962.

Our battalion was sent on training maneuvers at a fort about a thousand miles distant. We went through the standard exercise of convoying across several states, moving all our necessary military hardware and personnel to the new position. The battalion was assigned as a component of a Blue division, who waged mock war against a similar Red division. By whim of the Army, I found myself assigned as the communications officer for a Blue umpire group.

The war game proceeded for a week. As Blue maneuvered and moved about, sometimes in the middle of the night, or any other time chosen by its commanding general, Blue umpire group had to move with it. My small communications platoon had to keep Blue umpire commander in constant touch with umpire headquarters back on the main post.

A radio teletype message came in. Per standard operating procedure, it was encrypted and subject to authentication. It decrypted and authenticated properly:

> EXERCISE CANCELLED - - - - - -
> ALL FORCES RETURN TO BASE

The Blue umpire commanding officer was a full colonel ... I, a lowly first lieutenant. My throat twitched. I gulped. Colonels are suspected of consuming lieutenants as snack food when angered. I asked for retransmission. While I watched my radio operators, the second transmission likewise decrypted, authenticated, and repeated the message. This was not a joke. It was real. I gulped harder.

I went through another of my few communications channels, with the same result. I then approached the Blue Division communications officer and asked him to connect me to umpire headquarters by field telephone, over his division network. I spoke to umpire headquarters: the messages were authentic. I gulped a third time, yet harder, and presented the original message, printed on yellow teleprinter paper, to my colonel.

He took a very dim view of a perceived joke. Rarely did I see more disgust toward a lower officer than that from him at that time. "This had !@#$ well better not be a JOKE!" he bellowed. I assured him that, to the best of my knowledge and ability, it was not. I had already set up a circuit for him to talk directly with umpire headquarters, and he did so. Then he set into action, ordering Blue Division to knock down and return to base. The field training exercise came to an abrupt end.

That Sunday evening President Kennedy addressed the nation.

The Cuban Missile Alert was 'ON.'

The Army was now called to full performance. This was not a drill.

Things moved at a dizzying pace. I was whisked away at 2 A.M. and returned to my home base one thousand miles distant by commercial air. My usual communications platoon was 'hot' and received top priority. Authorized to have 49 men at full staffing, it had eighteen, and nineteen vehicles. I had unfilled requisitions for maintenance spares inherited from the previous platoon leader! We were in no shape to do anything.

We were reassigned to the post signal field maintenance facility, a repair depot run by a really capable civilian. We were his top priority. He took our unfilled requisitions, spoke strange authentication code numbers into his telephone, and signal depots Lexington and Tobyhanna sent materials ... lots of materials ... quickly ... by special dispatch military aircraft and other means.

In that day a 'rush' order shipment was called 'Blue Streak.' Such a package had a big blue lightning bolt on each face. No matter how it was set down, those bolts were conspicuous ... very conspicuous. A supply center, on receiving one, had four hours to move it toward its final destination. Our company supply room began to fill up with lightning bolts. I stationed two of my men and a truck there, and we took possession of those packages, moving them to our storage areas. They were almost all maintenance spare parts.

Our storage area filled to the brim. I ordered that further packages be held at the company supply building. Our poor supply sergeant had conniptions! He needed to move those blue lightning bolts off his floor, and now! So, the supply officer and I, both lieutenants and personal friends, simply used a long strip of cloth 'engineer' tape down the center of his supply building, and labeled one side 'company supply' and the other 'communications platoon.' My men simply signed for packages as they were tossed across the tape. Everyone was happy.

The missile alert went on for a few months, and then abated. However, my maintenance spare parts kept arriving. My main communications wagon, a semi-trailer van, contained four full radio-teletype operating positions, complete with cryptographic machines. The machines were of an older type. My van was whisked away from me and taken to a field depot where the old crypto machines were replaced with the latest and greatest. When it was returned to me, I, the officer in charge, was NOT cleared by security to enter the equipment van. I had no crypto clearance, but was asked to sign for, and be responsible for, the van and its contents. I refused.

I was crypto cleared in two weeks and took control of my van, full of equipment.

The Inspector General

Returning to the military's calisthenics-like exercises, the Army sent a team around to all its troop units once per year. This team was commanded by the inspector general. Our scheduled inspection date was approaching. We advised that we needed the name of the officer or person who would inspect my communications van with its latest and greatest, most classified crypto equipment. No answer was received in spite of weekly requests for a few months.

The inspection team came. They did their standard thing. Each man [3] had a rifle, canteen, ammo belt, etc., etc. The team assured each did, and that it was in good condition. Discrepancies were cataloged.

The team inspected all our vehicles, all our special equipment, checking it off against our unit's Table of Organization and Equipment, to assure we had everything we were supposed to have, and that it was in good condition. Discrepancies were cataloged.

---

[3] It was 1963. Women were not yet totally integrated into line units.

The team inspected all our mobile operating positions, all but one – my crypto-enabled van. The team had no authority to enter that equipment. We had special orders that only twenty-four of my platoon members and NO OTHERS were permitted access. We had authority for use of lethal force to enforce these rules. We kept a round-the-clock, two-man guard with live ammunition positioned at the equipment, and the van was kept behind a secure fence.

On the team's last day of inspection, the inspector general himself, a one-star, said HE would conduct the inspections. We took him to the fenced compound, showed him the van, but insisted he was not permitted entry.

Anticipating a showdown, we had posted our best enlisted man as a guard outside the van, at the top of the external metal steps leading to its entry door. Our guard wore a red helmet, a red arm band, and carried a carbine, indicating to one and all that he had live ammunition and authority to use lethal force.

The general approached the van. The guard commanded, "Halt, Sir! I have orders to shoot to kill." And so he did. I had issued those orders!

The general disregarded the exhortation. He set foot on the first step. There was the unmistakable sound of a round being chambered. His advance was arrested by the carbine's muzzle against his breastplate. He looked up, saw the guard's steely-eyed, stern countenance, and backed down, face ashen, quite visibly shaken.

In a very short time he turned a rather deep, menacing red, and ordered all of us, guard included, to follow him to post headquarters. The group was composed of the guard, the company commander, the battalion commander, the general, and me. We had anticipated some sort of problem, and had a third guard on duty, to relieve the one who had accosted the general. We had come just short of killing a general – legally, of course.

We were ordered to post headquarters, the incident related to the two-star post commander, and a message was forwarded to Continental Army Command. We waited, standing at parade rest position, for a half hour. Finally came a reply:

Michael Toia

REFERENCE REQUEST TO INSPECT
COMMUNICATIONS VAN 519 SIGNAL
COMPANY

REQUEST DENIED REPEAT DENIED
  SIGNED
  COMMANDING GENERAL
  CONTINENTAL ARMY COMMAND

With that, the inspector general said, "Well, our boss's boss decided that you all did a fine job. Congratulations." And, he took his leave.

We all retired to our quarters, and some, including the company commander and I, showered off, did a necessary change of underwear and uniform, and then returned to work.

Milt

It once was by absolute good fortune my privilege to work under a magnificent supervisor. He was the laboratory director, and I, his deputy. His name was Milt.

In transit from my former employment in a distant state, my father passed away. I miss him. After the funeral and a few days of mourning, the new destination was reached and the new job got underway. It happened that Milt and I hit it off well, and seemed to develop a warm, father-son relationship. Milt's reaction appeared to be in accord with this assessment.

He was, on the outside, a rather unpretentious man, and though having lived in the area and worked at that laboratory for more than thirty years, retained his Mississippi-home accent and various speech mannerisms. However, his inner intelligence belied that outward simple country appearance. My career was well along by fifteen years; he was a marvelous mentor, and taught me much – technically, managerially, and just sheer wisdom about humanity.

He was approaching retirement age. Some two years into our working relationship, and after his getting me into the swing of the operation, Milt announced that he planned to retire. This gave me a twinge of sadness, yet happiness for him. Sadness came because I genuinely liked Milt, in fact loved him as does a son of a wonderful father. During our frequent daily discussions, I asked what he intended to do in retirement. He said he wanted to devote his time to gardening.

Our lab was out in the country, on a plot of a few hundred acres, and employees were permitted to have personal garden plots on the property. Many did so. On mine I grew tomatoes, peanuts, beans, and other assorted vegetables. Milt had nearly an acre of garden; it was his avocation. He lived in the nearby town, where his yard was heavily treed and hardly more than half an acre. Gardening was done at the lab.

Knowing this, I said, "Where are you going to garden?" He said he would just continue right at the lab. But I told him, once he is retired, he wouldn't be allowed to come onto the property, because of security and insurance issues. My true motive was simply not to lose his warm, wonderful friendship and mentoring.

He was taken aback. We discussed the matter on and off. He did not retire.

He made the same feint again the next spring. The same argument again brought him to a standstill. The second year he did not retire. The third spring we had the same discussion. But then he looked me directly in the eye, saw right down to my soul, and said, "You don't want me to retire, do you?"

I confessed, told him I truly cherished his presence, and it was so, then offered that he would always be welcome to come and garden as much as he wanted, and I hoped he would, daily, to continue having his guidance, mentoring, and friendship. That year Milt retired. And I truly did miss him, and do to this day.

We had many experiences together. The preponderance was quite educational, and I learned much. But there was one that caught this amazing man in a rather humorous position, and I relate it here.

Our lab had a limited budget. We were on a 'pecking order' list to acquire surplus government equipment. There was a NASA warehouse nearby, and we lived off a lot of NASA surplus. When a given space program was finished, usually with one satellite or another in orbit, NASA made its surplus parts available. A lot of it was special tooling, jigs, or assemblies of one sort or another. There was also general purpose test equipment, such as voltmeters, oscilloscopes, and the like that were useful to us. To obtain these, we had to take an entire lot of surplus material. We made good use of much of it.

One such shipment contained a wood pallet on which was a large metal ring, actually two metal rings held about a foot apart, and about 5 feet in diameter. There were a lot of shiny metal strips, like tape measures without markings, a lot of springs, and all apparently covered in something like brown mosquito netting. The whole shebang was laced crudely together with a large rope that encircled the assembly. This was too big to store indoors, so it sat in the rear parking lot for a time.

On my lunch stroll about the front of the property, the day balmy and pleasant, there rose a familiar voice from behind the building: "Help! Help!" Someone was in distress, and Milt was calling for assistance. I ran around the building and found the commotion. It was the pallet with the mosquito netting, metal rings, springs, and so on.

Milt, ever curious, decided that many of the hardware parts might be useful and had begun to remove that rope lacing, and when he got to a critical point, the assemblage began to expand! Those many springs began spreading the tape-measure steel strips out like the petals of a daisy, and the attached mosquito netting followed. The netting began deploying itself. The sole force limiting the expansion was a human body spread-eagle on the pile. It was Milt!

I looked, and said, "What the …?"

But he implored, "Get help!"

I ran into the laboratory building, picked up the rear door phone, dialed the intercom, and said, "All hands on deck! Emergency in the rear parking lot. Everyone who can spare ten minutes, report at once."

The lab began emptying into the parking lot. We saw Milt. People started to giggle, then to laugh out loud, and every time Milt moved or twitched, that mosquito netting grew. It now engulfed half a nearby pickup truck. I started to give directions as to pushing the netting back to its original place, but one of our engineers said, "Hold everything! I have exactly the right tool. I'll be right back." He came back with a camera and tripod. He photo-documented Milt's predicament.

It didn't take long after to get the mess back onto the pallet, under control, and tied up, with Milt extricated from its innards. Being the person he was, he saw the humor of the situation, and laughed the best about it. He was just that sort of a man, that sort of a manager, and that's one reason we all loved him.

We later looked into the matter a bit, and found the device was a complete, operating, spare antenna parabolic reflector for the ATS-F satellite. When deployed in space, it was, I believe, over fifteen feet in diameter.

Miss ya, Milt. It's been decades. Rest in peace, my good friend and mentor.

Michael Toia

Security Interview

The Army assigned our platoon to a deeply secret operation. We needed some sort of special security clearance, so they scheduled the lot of us for sessions with the 'poly' operator, a nice fella, who operated a polygraph machine. You may know it as a lie detector.

Now, undergoing a poly exam is no big deal, depending on how honest or devious you are. Some classes of people – politicians, used car salesmen – are acknowledged pathological liars. There would be little emotional reaction to their statements, so the poly machine would simply hum along contentedly.

A good Catholic, it is said, has a terrible time of it. As a former Catholic and Christian, I have the same problem. We've been instructed from the time we are born that we are sinners, have done wrong, and must continually seek the Lord's forgiveness. Ask me to tell the truth under oath, and my mind races with thoughts such as: I think what I am about to say is true, but let me examine my thoughts in more detail. Just where was I last March 14th? Is my name really Michael? Did I ever tell someone, even kiddingly, that I was someone else? Did I ever use an alias?

The poly box picks up reactions to every one of these thoughts. Its pens wiggle back and forth. We sweat a bit.

SCRIBBLE SCRIBBLE!

We hesitate in breathing.

SCRIBBLE SCRIBBLE!
We twitch a tad.

SCRIBBLE SCRIBBLE!
Every little nuance of our bodily reaction goes

SCRIBBLE SCRIBBLE!
SCRIBBLE SCRIBBLE!
SCRIBBLE SCRIBBLE!

The damned machine reacts to our body language, and the more truthful we are, the worse it gets. For a confirmed liar, who can do so under oath, it doesn't react at all, but a really truthful person will run it out of ink in about three minutes.

My first time through such an interview caught me a tad off guard. The operator asked, "Do you advocate the violent overthrow of the government of the United States?"

Well, my reader, do you? Give it some thought ...

My father was a strict constitutionalist. He impressed that into my very fiber, and I dare say provided it directly in my genes.

The constitution, an interesting document the size of a pamphlet, grants the government certain restricted powers, and enumerates many of those restrictions. We may say any damned phrase we like, according to its first amendment ... "political correctness" or "PC" notwithstanding. In fact, PC is, under the most direct and simplest analysis, "CP" – constitutionally proscribed.

We are secure in our persons, papers, and effects against unwarranted search ... rights not granted to the government by that pamphlet are reserved to the states, or to the people.

The second amendment, like it or hate it, prohibits the government from infringing our right to keep and bear arms. Infringed is the word in the pamphlet ... an interesting term. Just where does infringement start, anyway? I won't delve further into that political and social minefield! Just recall the events preceding the constitution. British soldiers with arms were housed in our

Michael Toia

homes and on the land. The Unites States found King George's laws and regulations stiflingly oppressive. They took up arms and by that means beat the British off the soil of the colonies. Our founding fathers required their citizens to maintain the means to defend themselves against an oppressive government, anticipating that the need would one day again arise.

Now study history. It is the internal reaction of any government to disarm its people, thereby converting citizens to subjects. And, every government in the world takes to itself more and more power, drowning its subjects in what de Tocqueville termed quiet despotism. We have 2,000+ pages of an Affordable Healthcare Act, 7,000+ pages of a tax code, and on, and on …

Oh, yes … the Affordable Patient Healthcare "Tax" that our legislators carefully crafted as not a tax and our President, responsible for this thing, insisted is not a tax. Tell it to the judge. Come to think of it, you did – nine of them. *They* said it's a tax.

At what point does a subject rise up and again become a citizen, holding his or her government to account, and demand restrictions? Throughout history this has occurred time and again, quite often by force of armed revolution. My preferred manner would be by the several states calling a constitutional convention to amend the constitution, disband the office of a czarist president, and replace the executive with a five-person executive panel; disband and dismiss a bench-legislating Supreme Court; repeal various laws as need be, and severely prune the myriad choking tangle of government kudzu, rosa multiflora, and other poisonous weeds of regulation that proliferate daily, piling up above our knees, navels, chins, ears, and drowning us completely. Absent this, should a revolution break out and shooting begin, pitting constitutionalists against an abusive government, there is no doubt at all – I must be pulling the trigger as a constitutionalist. Were it not so, my father would rise from his grave and rightfully beat me into mine.

I remember one politician's statement: "It's impossible to love your country and hate your government." I guess he never really looked at a dollar bill, at the portrait thereupon, and gave his statement any thought. Oh, well … some are incapable of philosophical reflection in depth.

So, you have just waded through my bit of tirade above. How do you think that polygraph reacted? HA!

SCRIBBLE SCRIBBLE!   SCRIBBLE SCRIBBLE!
SCRIBBLE SCRIBBLE!   SCRIBBLE SCRIBBLE!
SCRIBBLE SCRIBBLE!   SCRIBBLE SCRIBBLE!
SCRIBBLE SCRIBBLE!   SCRIBBLE SCRIBBLE!

The poor thing near caught fire! Metaphorically speaking, screaming bloody murder, it leapt from its table, out the door, down the hall, outside, and shot across the parking lot. A short time later, a column of smoke could be seen in the distance, the wail of a fire engine permeating the air.

Nowadays, a poly operator and his machine seem to know me. I guess they simply have my life history at hand for review. That question is first asked with the machine off, we discuss my constitutional convictions, and it is re-phrased: "Do you advocate the violent overthrow of the constitutionally-empowered and limited government of the United States?"

The machine can actually be heard to exude a deep sigh of relief. It simply hums lightly along as I very contentedly and calmly answer, "No."

Ain't it nice that, with a bit of negotiating, life's trials can be reduced to such simple terms?

Michael Toia

Antenna Failure

A lot of interesting scientific and engineering work happens in East Central Florida, about the Cape Canaveral area. A radio communications engineer, I spent a good deal of my travel time there, working on various projects. One several-year development involved a new adaptation of the century-plus phenomenon of shortwave radio. We were developing a means for a large base station to communicate with a field station that was very small and highly portable.

Many meetings occurred, some running just a bit into the evening. On one occasion, we went quite late. Discussion centered on the computer programming aspects of the system, not my forte, but that of several experts in the room. As 9 P.M. approached, this thread had been going on for several tens of minutes. I listened.

I closed my eyes, went into a more relaxed state, and just rested until my expertise might again be needed. The discussion continued. Eventually came a longer period of quiet.

A colleague looked across the table at me, said, "Look at Mike over there. He looks like he's sound asleep! I bet the old dog is listening to every word we say."

Continuing my previous relaxed pose, eyes closed, I said, "I've merely shut down the video, gentlemen. Continue."

He said, "See! I told you so! I've been working with that guy for years and I've seen him do this before!"

The contractor had a steel antenna tower, about 75' high, with a large log periodic antenna at the top. These antennas look like an old TV aerial on steroids. A long boom held a number of horizontal aluminum tubes sticking out both sides, in this case, over twenty of them. The largest one was about sixty feet across. As the contract proceeded, we planned to use that antenna for on-the-air, whole system tests.

The experimental field station later was put together on a brass board, electrically fully functional, but not to final size. It was on a large metal plate, about thirty by forty inches, with everything screwed down onto that plate. This was put into a motor home with a lot of companion test equipment, and we were to take a few weeks to drive it from Florida to Washington State, stopping along the way to do tests and take measurements of performance. Everything was put together and at a few of those long meetings, we developed a test plan, the driving route, the number of test stops, and the logistics of all this. We developed a schedule, a rather complex calendar of events, and initiated the test calendar.

A week before the planned departure date, we had a call from the prime contractor. The test had to be postponed a few weeks.

Now, this involved re-scheduling several other contractors from different companies, and government employees from several agencies. There had better have been a good reason! So, the prime contractor offered one.

It seems that a lot of ocean shore birds, several pounds each, flocked toward the antenna. They perched on its long aluminum tubes. The weight was too great, the tube snapped off, its load of birds fluttering again to the wing to settle on the next tube. It, too, could not support the weight and snapped away. In not more than a half-hour the flock had pruned most of the tubes from the antenna that then laid in ruins – part still up on the tower, and the rest scattered on the ground beneath. It would take two weeks to effect the repair. The excuse was accepted.

Across the Might Miss

October, 1962. The 40th Signal Battalion (Pole Line Construction) was ordered to Fort Hood, Texas, for a multi-week exercise. I was its convoy's duly appointed "Class A Agent." I carried the cash [4] to pay for gasoline, meals, and expenses as our fifty-nine vehicles trundled across Georgia, Alabama, and approached Mississippi.

Now, if you study history, that was a time of federally-enforced integration of schools and colleges. There were a few tense situations in Alabama and Mississippi. In the former, the governor called out the National Guard to prevent enforced integration. The President simply drew the Alabama Guard into federal service, removing them from the governor's service and instead placing them into federal service, to help enforce integration.

We were federal troops. We traveled trans-Alabama without incident, and approached Mississippi, and at its gates were stopped by the Mississippi State Police. What were our intentions? What were our orders? Why were we trying to enter Mississippi?

---

[4] And a sidearm with live ammunition, with red arm band to signify use of deadly force was authorized.

The battalion commander presented our written orders: We were to report to Fort Hood, Texas, for maneuvers. US Route 80 ran from our home base in Georgia, through Mississippi, into Texas. It was our selected route.

The police chatted a bit on their radios. Then they ordered us to form up in closed convoy, and began escorting us along US 80, westbound, under their control. This accommodated our orders, and moving in closed convoy is safer and easier than in open, the difference being that open allows civilian traffic to intermingle with our vehicles, whereas closed keeps about 25 feet spacing between our vehicles, moving under police escort, and does not permit civilian traffic to intermingle. We moved as a solid block of Army vehicles.

Our orders were to overnight at the Meridian, Mississippi, Air Force Base. The police escorted us there, and assured that all of our vehicles were on the base. They guarded the entrance/exit all night long. We cared not: it did not interfere with our orders or timing.

Came morning and we discussed our plans with the police, and at 0600 hours began departing the base, again in closed convoy with police escort. We proceeded westbound on US 80, toward the bluffs at Vicksburg. Per our request, the police held us there, above the bluffs. At their base, lay the Vicksburg Bridge, across the Mississippi and into Louisiana.

It was a toll bridge.

As I was a Class A Agent, my driver took me to the toll operator. The bridge was old ... very old. The toll machine was old ... very old. It looked like a huge brass cash register of the time, with oversized buttons. Each button existed for a vehicle of a given classification, axle count, and weight. The toll operator was old ... very old. Likely, he was the first ever to operate the big brass machine. He was very experienced.

I had a list of each of our fifty-nine vehicles – axle count, weight, and classification. I showed it to the operator. He said, "Sonny, I've been doing this for a very long time. Just send your convoy down, and I'll count them, one at a time."

I got on my radio, gave the old man [5] the signal … "Roll 'em." Shortly a state police car approached the bridge, and peeled off. It was followed by the commander's jeep. I saluted. The convoy began its crossing, moving at thirty miles per hour.

"Sedan … two axles ... 25 cents," rang up on the big brass machine. A ¾-ton truck was only fifteen feet behind. "Truck … one ton … two axles ... 50 cents," rang up on the big brass machine.

A deuce and a half followed. "Truck … two ton … three axles

"75 cents," spake the machine.

Another deuce and a half … "Ditto," spake the machine.

Another deuce and a half … pulling a trailer load of telephone poles. "What was that?" asked the toll collector.

Following my list, I called out, "Deuce and a half, plus single axle trailer."

"What size trailer?"

"Dunno … two ton?"

Three more vehicles whizzed past during our discussion.

"Truck ... two ton ... three axles … 75 cents," spake the machine.

"Trailer ... two ton ... single axle ... 75 cents," spake the machine.

By then, we were three vehicles behind. The toll collector asked me what had followed the first truck and pole trailer.

"Same thing."

"Truck … two ton … three axles ... 75 cents," spake the machine.

"Trailer ... two ton ... single axle ... 75 cents," spake the machine.

Things began to unravel as four more vehicles zipped onto the bridge. We were now six behind, with which the operator agreed that my initial assessment was wise. We simply went over my list, and he rang up each and every vehicle on my inventory. Then the

---

[5] Battalion Commander

operator did a grand total: "Thirty seven dollars and fifty cents," spake the big brass machine. I drew that amount from my cash box and gave it to the operator. Then, per requirement, I asked for a receipt in triplicate. You'd have thought I asked for a piece of the moon! But, after considerable trouble and delay, I had my receipts. I walked across the way, got into my jeep, and told the driver, "Hit it." We rolled past the toll booth.

"Wait! I didn't get your vehicle!" shouted the old timer.

I waved "Ta - Ta" and away we went into Louisiana.

My convoy, per standard operating procedure, was rolling westward across Louisiana at 40 mph. It was nearly a half hour ahead of me. My driver put pedal to the metal, took the jeep's speedometer needle, and simply set it against the stop pin at 60 mph. We rolled for a full hour before I came across my five-ton, thirsty wrecker. Per procedure, we convoy-hopped, got ahead of the old man's jeep, and flew westbound in search of a gas stop.

I found a small town that had three gas stations, two on the right and one on the left. Each had a large sign:

WE GIVE S&H GREEN STAMPS. [6]

These had some cash value, and by order, I had to collect them and turn them into the post recreation room fund. Now, try traveling with a few thousand dollars' worth of S&H green stamps, in sheets about 10 by 12 inches, on your clipboard in an open-sided jeep during a rainstorm. Not nice. And, I would get royal #@!! from the post central fund for their condition when I returned home.

So, I distinctly asked each station manager, "You DO NOT give green stamps to military convoys, DO YOU?"

And we came to agreement ... they did not.

I hit the radio. "I've arranged a gas stop. Speedometer reading per my speedometer." The old man knew the offset between his

---

[6] In that era, many merchants participated in a program where they gave a customer "green stamps," not unlike postage stamps, with gummed backs. These were collected and pasted into a small book by the customer and could be redeemed for useful merchandise; 2,500 stamps for a toaster, 750 for a screwdriver set, 1,500,000 for a Cadillac ...

and mine, so he knew within a mile where I was. Yes, this was prior to GPS.

My vehicles began to file into the three stations. My driver and the old man's driver served as traffic cops to direct each vehicle to the right station and pump ... and we gassed up.

In a convoy, the mechanics' ¾-ton truck was always last, directly behind the wrecker. Mechanics' orders were never to pass by a convoy vehicle and leave it stranded. So, as the convoy re-formed, all gassed up, my driver and I held behind to pay the final bill. A young teen-ager was pumping gas into the wrecker's tank under the driver's running board. Pump. Pump. Pump. And the pump went Ding! Ding! Ding!

He stopped, looked at the truck, and looked under it. The drive said, "Fill it, boy. Keep pumping." Ding! Ding! Ding! went the pump.

The tank had a 55-gallon capacity. The wrecker was always the pacing vehicle in a convoy as it usually was towing something else that had broken down along the road. It was the thirstiest of the lot. Its tank was damned near empty at each stop. I had to know its approximate mileage endurance, and used that to select gas stops.

Finally the boy filled the tank. He looked at the gas pump ... $15.50 ... Wow! [7]

The driver said, "C'mon, son ... fill the one on the other side."

Yes, the M55 wrecker had twin 55-gallon tanks.

The poor boy near fainted!

---

[7] Gas then was about 30 cents per gallon ... believe it or not!

Don and Doctor Bob

In the course of a career one sometimes changes occupation, pursues one's deeper interests. My avocational fascination, brought about by the hobby of ham radio that I entered at age 14, was, is, and shall remain, radio antennas. These seemingly simple bits of wire and metal tubes somehow allow one to hear, and furthermore communicate with, people all over the world, as far away as Europe and Australia. It just seems like magic!

One day a vacancy announcement crossed my desk: "Wanted - Antenna Engineer. Voice of America, Washington, DC." I applied. A time later the antenna engineering section had me in its fold. I was now an engineer with Voice of America, or VOA.

We were led by a pleasant fellow, a PhD, quite knowledgeable, whose first name was Robert. He came to be known – affectionately – as Dr. Bob, after the Muppets character. The term was meant in respect, and he took it that way. However, over a year that respect faded.

VOA is an interesting place, and working on one's fascination was just amazing. It was one of the best jobs I had had to that time. The first two weeks were devoted to writing an engineering standard that absolutely had to be in the contracting office on a due date, some fifteen days hence. We worked in small teams, two of us cooperating heavily for two weeks straight, starting before 8:30 A.M. and running until past 10:00 P.M., weekends included. When we two completed the work late on the eve of the Monday due date, I personally punched and comb-bound the required six copies, and set them on my chair. We then ran from the office after 10:30 P.M. and just caught the very last metro train out of town toward our homes.

Monday came. The requisite six copies were delivered before the 10:00 A.M. due time. Then we set about cleaning up the papers, reference volumes, punchings, computer printouts, etc. in our offices so we could get down to more routine work. I had come to VOA as a government employee with ample leave time on the books. I took Tuesday off.

Friday, the timekeeper asked me how I was to account for Tuesday. I told her we had just worked 'round the clock for fifteen days, and it should be compensatory time. She advised that Dr. Bob had not entered any paperwork for this extra time. I charged the day off to annual leave, a somewhat sour taste set into my psyche.

Not long after, as I entered the office suite, Dr. Bob said that a contract had just been let to develop an antenna, and the contract needed a 'Contracting Officer's Technical Representative,' known everywhere as a COTR except at VOA, where they called them 'ARCOs' – Authorized Representatives of the Contracting Officer. I was puzzled; we hadn't solicited a request for any such thing. Dr. Bob said the proposal was unsolicited; we needed an ARCO and tag … I was it.

I met the contractor, read the contract, the technical details, etc. Then, on return to our office suite, Dr. Bob's supervisor, Don, accosted me in the hall next to the elevators. Backing me against the wall and jabbing his right index finger into my left shoulder blade to the point of pain, he told me in no uncertain terms, that contract should never have been let, and my future at VOA depended on how I killed it.

You may talk about a veiled threat. This was not. This was veil-less. The tongue lashing I received from Don, unexpected and not in any way my fault, sent me reeling. Thank God it was Friday.

Michael Toia

A weekend of anguished soul-searching brought the conclusion – I was a professional engineer, so I would handle the contract accordingly, in a professional style. I would look for employment elsewhere post haste.

Contracts required personal visits by the ARCO to the contract facility. I discussed the matter with the contractor's principle investigator. He was quite concerned. He asked me what I had decided, and I told him. Don resigned two weeks later. Corporations have a big, talented legal staff, and own a few congressmen and senators, I guess.

Someone in the office, a mole, put me dead center in the sights of a headhunter – a professional recruiter who tries to 'sell' talented individuals to corporations. My phone began to ring, ring, ring. The fellow would not let up. Finally, to call off his dogs, I agreed to an interview. I was forty-nine. Who hires forty-nine year old engineers?

The corporation made an offer! I was stunned! I thought it over, but had about seventeen years of service with the government, so turned them down. This did what I thought it might; the headhunter stopped calling, he called off his dogs.

Moreover, a strange thing happened. The corporate manager who wanted to hire me called me. He said, "Sir, I need you now. I needed you two years ago. I will need you two years from now. Please write down my name and phone number, keep it in your wallet, and if you change your mind, give me the first right of refusal to hire you." Well, I was quite taken aback and rather flattered, so I did as he asked.

Then came the time for an annual review. One could receive one of five ratings: Outstanding, Highly Successful, Successful, Needs Improvement, and Unsuitable. I received a 'Successful.' It's the only time in my life to be rated that low. It stung. It stung badly.

I talked to Dr. Bob about it. He said I produced a PhD thesis a week, and can have an outstanding rating anytime I want. The rules were: work 40 to 60 hours a week … Successful, work 60 to 80 hours a week … Highly Successful, or work over 80 hours a week … Outstanding – if the work was of a high caliber. I said I had a wife and two little girls and couldn't shortchange them by working over 80 hours a week. He had the unmitigated gall to sit at his desk, smile at me while tapping the four fingers and thumb of one hand against those of the other, and said I needed to decide which was more important ... job or family?

Well ... *that* took three milliseconds.

Steamingly angry, I stalked back to my desk. The adrenalin was still flowing as the phone rang. It was the headhunter. I hadn't heard from him in a few months. I surmise the office 'mole' was Dr. Bob. The headhunter tried to convince me I really ought to take that job. I said, "Okay, tell them I accept their offer." He apparently didn't grasp that, and continued with his sales pitch. I repeated the statement again, and a third time.

Then he stopped and said, "What are you saying?"

I said, "Tell them I accept their !#@#$%!! offer!" with profanity injected as indicated.

It didn't take more than a half hour for my phone to ring again, this time after the adrenaline rush. It was the corporate manager. We came to terms. It was August, and I would start December first.

He said, "That's quite a lapse. Is there a reason?"

I said, "Yes. I am handling a contract that is going well, and I expect to finish it on time and on budget, and get more quality from its product than we had expected. I want to finish it. It concludes November 30."

After a short quiet spell, he said, "That's the best reason I've ever heard. I'll see you at 8 A.M. December first."

And, that's how I left the employment of Voice of America – an interesting place to work, whose managers are the worst I've ever seen. If they ever offer you a job, and you are starving, take it. Otherwise, tell them where they can shove it.

World's Biggest Computer

This is a standard story told over many years. I was about twenty when I first heard it, and, as with so many stories, its attribution is unknown to me. It is 'anon.'

World governments convene frequently in Geneva to work out scientific treaties and standards related to international cooperation. Under the International Telecommunications Union there is a radio committee, ITU-R; a telegraph and telephone committee, ITU-T; and so forth. One such committee met in plenary session. It appointed a working group to study and advise on a computer with increased power and speed. The working group presented its recommendation, that all nations of the earth combine resources to build this computer. It was to be rather like 'Deep Thought' in Douglas Adams' "Hitchhiker's Guide to the Galaxy." It was to be the world's biggest computer.

The plenary session considered the proposal long and dutifully. By and by, the member countries agreed. The working group then began assessing how to do this, and its ranks grew to have members from each of the cooperating countries. Big, heavy-duty processing core machines were to be built in many places: Japan, France, Germany, etc. etc. They were to be put into close communication by world-spanning fiber optic cable. The hundreds of millisecond delay through satellites would be too slow.

A data base subcommittee convened to consider the big machine's data base. It should have ready access to the sum total of human knowledge: medicine, theology, politics, history, science, mathematics, and on, and on. There was such a task just to compile the data base and put it into acceptable digital format. That took a few years in itself to complete.

A hardware subcommittee convened to lay out the large computer rooms and decide which country could house which one. They fought Moore's law, which states computer power and speed seems to double every eighteen months. The subcommittee's work spanned a few of these Moore-gaps.

A communications subcommittee convened to design the data links necessary to provide the massively-parallel processor machine the ability to exchange data and algorithmic tasks. A software subcommittee convened to consider how best to make efficient use of the massively-parallel architecture. In all, it took eight years, but at last the machine was built, linked, data base loaded, software tested, and ready for tasking.

The plenary session reconvened. They discussed at great length: what should we ask this machine? It should be capable of providing great insight and wisdom, as it could consult every fact known to man. They worked for several weeks on this single question. It was rather like the question put to Deep Thought: What is the answer to life, the universe, and everything? [8]

Finally they came to agreement. The machine's first question would be: Is there a god?

The local operator, working from a control terminal at the plenary session, dutifully brought the great machine to operation, and posed the question. Then video feeds displayed activity at the various machine locations in the many countries. Machine rooms hummed. Lights blinked, flashed, and twinkled. Great communication modems showed flashing lights indicating strenuous activity, as data flowed to and fro. Individual video monitors in

---

[8] Forty-two, according to Adams' novel.

the multiple local control rooms flashed various and multiple messages by the screen full, and this activity continued for three and a half hours.

Finally things returned to the quiescent state, rather quickly. Frenzied blinking banks of lights settled to a slow, steady pattern. The monitors in all the scattered computer equipment rooms announced an end to the activity and returned to a 'ready' state. Communication modems settled down to an 'idle' state. The great machine had calculated an answer! Its output was communicated to the plenary session control operator's console.

In answer to the question, "Is there a god?" ... The great machine's monitor displayed: "There is NOW."

Snow

Living in the Northeast you expect winter snow. It happens. Many a beautiful scene contains billions of freshly fallen flakes draped as a blanket over the bushes, trees, as coverings on walkways and roadways, rendering parked autos as giant white-capped mushrooms. Such is the stuff of picture postcards and Christmas cards. The scenes are truly beautiful. On an early Friday afternoon the flakes appeared, slowly at first, then mustering more and more of their minions. They began arriving in earnest. By early Saturday, they formed a ten-inch deposit in the yard and on the driveway. Everything was so beautiful, pristine, fresh.

But, the flakes forgot to stop.

As nightfall approached, they had accumulated to a depth of fifteen inches. Yet, they continued. The sky proceeded to shed itself of its cold burden. The depth increased. Near 2 A.M. multitudes had joined forces and attacked a large tree standing along the main highway. The tree sought support, tried to lean on the main power line serving our village, but it was too little, too late. It surrendered, came crashing down onto the road, which was not passable at that time anyway. The line came down with the tree. Our lights went out. The village's lights went out.

This is always an inconvenience, the more so as our water supply came from a well whose pump then ceased to do its duty. We were without water. And the furnace, fueled with gas, was a rather modern unit, with fancy electrical and electronic controls, all of which then also ceased in their mission. The house chilled. It got cold. We were without heat, without water.

The kitchen's gas range was also rather modern, with electronic controls and ignition, so ceased to function normally. Thankfully, it could be ignited with a common match, and the oven thereof provided what little heat could be had. We took up residence nearby. Water was obtained by the simple act of baking snow and cooking it down on the stovetop burners. As it formed, it was poured into one of two large buckets for later use.

A phone call for help found that the entire village was suffering similarly. Our eight hundred foot driveway through a stand of woods and by a patch of bamboo was not passable. We called to have it plowed, but no one could service us for several days. We remained stranded.

The flakes continued their accumulation throughout Saturday, and finally at Sunday sunup the sky had exhausted its supply. The storm ceased. The sun came out bright, revealing a twenty-three inch blanket of beautiful snow, which held us in its grip. We surveyed the scene, took note of our situation. Plows had been heard clearing the road on which we lived. A small snow shovel, the only one we owned, was put into service, and by Sunday sunset we had dug a two-foot wide path down the driveway about two hundred feet, to the bamboo patch. Only six hundred feet to go! The bamboo had been pulled down into a tangled mess across the driveway. I worked it with a small hand pruning saw and cut a path through it.

We approached the telephone again. No dial tone. It had failed. Service was provided by Verizon FIOS, through a little box outside the house, powered by a small internal battery kept charged from the normal household electricity. The battery ran out. We realized then that our cell phone still functioned, but knew its battery would eventually die as well. Our two daughters lived nearby; we called and updated them about our situation.

Michael Toia

Sunday evening power was restored to the village. We could see the normal lights, but our home remained dark. The high line down our lane fed but a single house ... ours. We realized our priority to obtain full service had fallen to the very bottom of the list, and knew it would be several days.

Monday digging out of the pathway continued. The cell phone battery ran out. Thankfully, in my shop was a 12-volt to 110-volt inverter that produced normal household current from a car battery. This worked from our auto, and permitted a recharge of the cell phone. At least we were yet able to communicate. Our digging advanced another two hundred feet.

The girls called. They were now able to take to the roads, and were coming to our aid. An hour or so later, they were at the road end of the driveway and could hail us. We returned the shouts. Both parties continued the dig out. Quite exhausted by the long, strenuous hours, I turned to my wife with whom the single shovel was shared in working shifts and said, jokingly, "Two girls! You gave me two girls! I needed boys, several of them. But no, you had to provide girls." She laughed, and then said to stop complaining and keep digging.

In a few hours we had advanced to within a hundred feet of the girls' path descending from the road. I wondered how much longer it would take to dig out, and where we might stay until our power was restored. Various small plow trucks negotiated the area, and an occasional Department of Transportation plow would pass by. Then a work truck from the power company came by. I hoped they would stop and restore our service. The girls heard it coming, and saw it approach. They stationed themselves along the road, waved and batted their eyelashes, exuding that quality women possess that men find irresistible.

The truck stopped! Its driver stepped out. The girls explained that Mom and Dad, both in their sixties, were stuck, without power since Saturday morning, and needed help. The driver, a lineman, walked down their path, then pushed his way through the snowdrifts, examining our high line. He approached our position. We talked. I said the line was intact from this point to the house, and he could see that it was. Returning to his truck, he deployed a hotstick, pulled the fuse from the pole at the road end of the driveway, and replaced it. Power came on! The girls thanked him. We were still about a hundred feet from the road, shoveling away.

Later that afternoon we had a walking path from house to road. We had prepared for the predicted storm by parking one auto nearby, just off the road, and the four of us working together dug it out. We had transportation.

I apologized to my wife. Boys? Who needs boys? One beautiful girl can redirect a thousand to accommodate her wishes, and she gave me a pair of them.

We returned to a warm, cozy home, exhausted, thankful, and had a good night's sleep.

Honey

When I first laid eyes on her, she took my breath away. That sweet, shy, demure young lady cast an inescapable spell, and in a few short months we married. I was then, and today – more than a half century later – remain totally in love with my bride.

Then we were young. Shortly after the wedding, we found ourselves in Georgia as I, a new Army officer, began serving my country.

Georgia is a beautiful state. We lived in near-poverty, but I was amazingly happy as I had my precious with me. The state has its unique customs, mannerisms, and dialect that we found fascinating; we rather fell in love with the place.

Now, my army pay was the princely sum of two hundred twenty-two dollars and thirty cents a month. In addition, the base had no on-post housing, so we lived out in the general populace, I reporting to duty each day while my sweet went about life among the local population. I worked with many others from all across the country. It was rather like a United Nations gathering when it came to dialects of the English language –Western, Bostonian, Hoboken-ish, Southern, and so forth. One's ears became accustomed to hearing English pronounced in many differently accented forms.

After many months, we returned for a Christmas visit to our family home in Western Pennsylvania. The drive was long, so we took turns. The last several-hour shift into the early morning was mine, as my darling slept with her head on my shoulder. She had a busy day planned, helping with the extended family meal and holiday preparations. We arrived about 3 A.M. and quickly bedded down for the night.

About eight o'clock the following morning, a commotion rousted me from a deep sleep.

I heard the excited voices of my mother, mother-in-law, sister-in-law, and a few nieces. Just what the heck was the problem? I stepped into my pants, went out the door and down the hall, and there the family female contingent was assembled, in the midst of all preparations for a sumptuous holiday meal.

It seems my sweetheart had ignited some sort of unwanted attention. Now, she was always so soft, meek, and what one calls a 'shrinking violet.' She never did, and never does, like attention. That's undoubtedly one of the many features that attract me to her; I love it.

The chorus from the family females was, "Oh, listen to Joyce! She sounds like a Southern Belle! It's beautiful!"

Now, did I mention that my love liked attention? I don't think so … exactly the opposite. She took refuge by burying her face into my bosom, holding on to me tightly, and I held her as tenderly as I could.

With tears in her eyes, in that half-tempo cadence characteristic of Southern living, and with that oh-so-sweet Georgia female accent, she said, "Ho-ney … they-all saay ah sound lak ah Southern Belle! Now, ah don't now, do ah, ho-ney?"

Well, you just had to hear her! It was absolutely beautiful and sooooo sweet, dripping honey from every syllable, that it would melt the hardest of hearts. I had been living in Georgia with her for many months, and had become accustomed to her gradual change in dialect, and had not noticed it, other than perhaps to fall even more deeply in love with her. But now, back North of the Mason-Dixon Line, and having an ear recalibration from the immediate family, I realized how Joyce had turned to Honey. Marvelous!

Several months later, my commitment in Georgia ended, and we move to New Jersey. Honey lost that wonderful accent in three short days. More's the pity. But her voice would still melt your heart … it does mine every day.

Love ya, Honey.

Poof!

The Boy Scout experience is a good one for young boys, and ours was so. Living in a small mill town not far from Pittsburgh in Western Pennsylvania, we learned to spell the state name watching trainload after trainload of coal or iron ore creep by the local railroad crossings on their way to the blast furnaces or coke ovens. The railroad name was the same, and letters about two feet high appeared on the side of each gondola. There it was ... on four adjacent panels: P E N   N S Y   L V A   N I A. We always remembered it as twelve letters, four groups of three.

I digress. This story is about scouting, and a particular episode thereof. Our local troop met in the basement of the Methodist Church, and was led by a magnificent gentleman who took time from his busy work schedule to mentor the motley crew of us, molding and leading us into young manhood.

The hills at the edge of town held goodly amounts of plain, ordinary woods. Lots of trees, small streams, small cliffs of shale and sandstone, many springs, worked-out small sandstone quarries, and a few neglected, previously farmed, open fields were within. Our troop spent many a day out there – hiking , cooking, building small dams on the streams, exploring, and generally partaking in healthy air and exercise.

Weather was not often a detriment. Scoutmaster took us out at least one weekend a month. Other times we explored alone or in small groups of a few fellow scouts. It seemed that every boy of age eight to sixteen was a member of the local troop ... our town was not a large metropolis.

During one small expedition, we happened upon an oddity. The hills were pocked with oil wells dating from before the '29 stock market crash. No new ones had been drilled in that area since. The old ones still pumped, and produced oil. They were rather neat marvels of engineering, driven by a 'one-lung' gas engine, that is, a single cylinder engine much like a lawn mower, but bigger. They had pistons about twelve inches in diameter that moved through a stroke of about the same, a lawnmower piston about one-quarter that size.

These two-cycle engines were horizontal, had a piston rod exiting the base through an oil-lubricated gland, burned the wellhead natural gas, and had an outer water jacket cooled by wellhead brine, a natural antifreeze and, again, a product of oil wells. As they operated, about one to two strokes per second, they emitted a characteristic sound. They slowly sped up, until they inhaled more air than gas and began misfiring and slowed. A three-foot diameter flywheel kept them moving through the misfires.

We camped out, and many a time could hear them speak through the night:

Chuf.....Chuf....Chuf...Chuf..Shhh..Shhh...Shhhh....Shhhhhh

Chuf.....Chuf....Chuf...Chuf..Shhh..Shhh...Shhhh....Shhhhhh

Chuf.....Chuf....Chuf...Chuf..Shhh..Shhh...Shhhh....Shhhhhh

over and over, each firing a 'Chuf,' each misfire a 'Shhhh.' Their song oft lulled us to sleep rather nicely.

Now the oddity. We came across a shale-bedecked hillside, and there, partially exposed, lay a three inch diameter iron pipe, rusted, bespeaking its advanced age, one of the small pipelines connecting the wells to a pumping station in the valley below.

Michael Toia

We looked,. We were young. Our hearing was good. There seemed to be an almost imperceptible small hissss in the air. Then, moving a bit of the shale, we found it – the pipe had a hairline crack in it, a few inches long. This particular line apparently transported natural gas from the well field to the pumping station, to power its engines.

Not only were we young, but boys, and at great risk of repeating myself, foolish. Our first reaction, a twinge of fright, yielded to intrigue, then mild excitement. Scouts being ever prepared, one of us produced a match, lit it, and tossed it toward the crack ... and you can imagine what happened!

But, it did not. The pressure was so high that the leak simply blew out the match, and flung its carcass about ten feet down the hillside. Well! This was an unexpected result. We tried a few more matches, with much the same result.

Then it occurred to us. Pile some shale about the leak. Then try to light it. And lo! We had a nice gas burner, about like the large one on the kitchen stove. Its extinguishment then became a topic of the experience.

One of us simply kicked the shale off the crack. The fire blew itself out.

Aha! We had discovered a neat way of making a camp cooking fire. It was not a romantic wood fire, with embers, glow, smoke, and all the nice things of a fire pit, but it ought to be good for cooking. On later revisits to the site, we established that it was so. Our small group did not share this great find with others: we selfishly wanted it to be available for our own use on demand.

Came an early February day. Our troop had a planned outing into the woods. It had snowed the night before; rain, then snow. It was wet, soggy, miserable, and cold. A light fog enshrouded the town, the woods. But Scoutmaster said we would go, and go we did.

We reached an area about a mile out, a good campsite among the trees, and began setting up for our noon meal. Two of us decided we might try for our second-class scout fire-building and cooking merit badge. The shale-buried pipe was close by, so off we went, set up camp, piled shale over the crack, and began building a teepee fire atop the shale, using local wood. Everything was soaked. Not only had it rained, and then snowed the night before, it had rained all week. Nevertheless, we had announced our plan to Scoutmaster. He frowned on the idea, saying it took a really expert in scouting to build a cook fire under these conditions, but we said we wanted to try.

Finding the most miserable, rotted, and wet wood available, we constructed the teepee. Rotted wood behaves a bit like a sponge, and if one squeezed any of ours, the water would simply run out. In fact, just looking at the small teepee pile evinced water trying to run off the rotted wood.

We summoned Scoutmaster. He took one look at our 'fire,' said we were wasting his and our own time, and turned to walk off. We protested ... don't we get to try with two matches for the second class exam? He agreed ... and waited. My buddy produced one match, one of those larger wooden ones prepared ahead of time by having its head dipped in paraffin to waterproof it. He peeled off the paraffin coat, struck the match on a proper surface, and reached it toward the teepee.

And then, POOF! Our cook fire lit ... just like at home in the kitchen. The scoutmaster looked, a bit of amazement and humor swept across his face, then a stern look. "You fail," He said. "You're not allowed to use accelerants to start the fire." We agreed. To us it was an impossible task under the weather conditions.

Alas, we also failed our cooking exam, as we had used an unauthorized fire. But it was fun. We were some of the few to have a cook fire that day, cook a decent meal, dry out some clothing, and warm up a bit.

Michael Toia

Spats

Our project was aligned with a discipline of earth and astronomical sciences shared between two universities. Very sensitive chemical and physical techniques can reveal tiny traces of differing minerals in various rock samples. This often employed means to look at traces of radioactivity in materials, and "space rocks" – meteorites and tektites – contain traces of radioactivity brought on by their exposure to cosmic radiation while in deep space before falling to earth. Their radioactivity dies away when they land on earth, and some dies away more quickly than others.

The atmosphere absorbs and changes the character of cosmic rays considerably. Space rocks of known arrival date on earth allowed our researchers to extract valuable information about interstellar conditions, and fresh finds – meteorites recently fallen to earth – were prize samples because of their unique radioactive fingerprints. To analyze these samples, we operated several radiation counter devices, similar to Geiger counters, in laboratory rooms throughout the building.

A new object would be chemically "digested" in baths of nitric or hydrochloric acid. The building reeked of the latter. Most metal items developed a quick coating of corrosion because of it. As a maintenance engineer, I spent a good deal of time removing this crust of chloride-rust, cleaning items, and applying liberal amounts of light oil on all exposed metal surfaces.

The acid environment attacked other materials as well. Our labs housed banks of electronic counting equipment. Each had an electrical cord needing an outlet to accept it. There were a number of "cube taps" distributed about, those single-plug to three-way outlet expanders commonly used. Many were made of a hard rubber-type material. The acidic fumes apparently attacked that rubbery stuff. It slowly hardened and lost its softer feel, but seemed to function properly ... until one day.

The morning's maintenance rounds had just been completed. I sat at my desk, updating the daily systems' status logbook. A department secretary came to my office, to report smoke coming from our counting lab on the second floor. This was not initially alarming, as sometimes a small electrical transformer in the equipment would overheat, begin its death throes, burn internally, yield smoke, and finally blow a fuse. But, it did need attention. A slight diversion in morning duties was in order.

Re-entrance to the lab revealed an entire wooden shelf supporting much electronic equipment in flames! I was able to pull the main circuit breaker, pull the local fire alarm, and attack the fire with the carbon dioxide extinguishers we kept available for the purpose. The fire department arrived in short order and completed the job.

Inspection revealed that one of those cube taps had deteriorated, overheated, caught fire, and sparked the blaze. The acid fumes had done quite a job, and taught yet another lesson: watch those cube taps carefully, re-wire the lab, and eliminate as many as possible.

Josh, a young man and senior student working part time as a lab assistant, did a lot of routine work under the direction and watchful eye of our research staff. One of his tasks was to make up routine batches of digestion fluid, in about 100-liter lots. These were mixed in a large polyethylene container, much like a garbage pail, mounted on castors for easy transportation about the area. He would first fill one to a marked level with water from the building distilled water main. Then he would don protective clothing – a lab apron, eye protection shield, and polyethylene gloves – and begin slowly adding the proper amount of concentrated acid to the mix; and on one day, it was a nitric acid mix.

He admitted the proper amount of water to a polyethylene container, reached for the large glass carboy of concentrated acid, and lo! Lost his grip. The carboy fell to the stone bench top and broke, throwing concentrated nitric acid about the lab. Josh spun immediately about, put his arm through a large pull ring of an emergency drench shower, and we became aware of the situation as the dispensed fifty gallons per minute began pouring into the main hall. These emergency showers had no floor drain. They were for emergencies only.

Josh was thoroughly washed down. Someone manipulated the shower manual shut off valve to stem the tide. Nitric acid had splashed onto his lab pants beneath the apron, and some onto the sleeves of his lab jacket. The shower performed its function well, rapidly diluting the acid, and Josh suffered only very minor acid attack to his skin, leaving the tell-tale yellow stain here and there. At least there was no serious damage. As a precaution, he was sent to the dispensary for medical assistance, and reappeared a few hours later in a lab coat and pants. His originals were rather dissolved by the acid, as was some of his undergarment. We sent him home for the day.

He had been wearing heavy leather work boots, and oddly they showed no ill effects from their acid encounter. After washing them thoroughly, he found he could still wear them to work, and did so. After all, they were comfortable and safe – industrial wear contrasted to everyday shoes.

One day a few months later, there had been a spill of something on the lab floor, and it left a spot that was rather sticky. As one walked across it, footwear tended to adhere to the floor and heralded the same with a "sqweenk … sqweenk … sqweenk" sequence, one per footstep.

Josh came to the lab, walked about, and crossed the patch. Two 'sqweenks' later, he stopped abruptly, a sudden somewhat surprised expression on his face. He looked at his feet. The bottoms of his work boots were behind him, one pace away, stuck to the floor, and their tops stayed in place about his ankles, as a pair of leather spats. He stepped away, in his spatted stocking feet, and went over to a nearby lab stool to sit and examine his socks. The boot bottoms still remained behind on the sticky patch.

We then decoded the problem. Although the leather survived the nitric acid quite well, the boots' cotton stitching apparently did not. And, with the sticky provocation, the stitching decided to give way. Perhaps it's a good thing, too, for the treatment of cotton by nitric acid produces a nice explosive: guncotton. Josh might have had a different experience by and by, perhaps a variant of a hotfoot?

Michael Toia

Casino

Some years back, we floated along on a week-long Caribbean cruise. Now, if you've ever had the experience, you know ... it's not a place for 'the biggest loser' – the TV show where people of considerable girth compete to see who loses the most of it in a set time. It's also not for strict dieters, or anyone on a diet designed for any purpose other than to gain weight, five pounds a week about guaranteed.

One wakes for pre-breakfast coffee, donuts, etc, on the aft deck, hastens to one's stateroom to prepare for formal breakfast, and is off to the main dining room. Then, on a stroll by the open breakfast bar, touches up on more coffee and yummies, brunch if desired, a second trip to the dining room for the noon formal meal, mid-afternoon munchies poolside, and the third trip for formal dinner. Following that, there are more goodies in the lounges and, of course, the midnight gala. The schedule affords little sleep until waking so as not to miss pre-breakfast the next morning ... and so go the days. As the comic Kelly Monteith once said, "Why, the whole *ship* is edible!"

One need also be forewarned about the johns. They do not flush slowly, with the characteristic whirlpool-type swirl. Rather, they are power assisted, and operate with a concomitant loud 'swoosh' noise. Men are advised to stand before flushing, so as not to incur injury to delicate anatomical extremities, and are also wise to keep a proper separation betwixt the bowl's rim and the wristwatch to maintain possession of same. It is rumored that on one occasion, an expensive Rolex was so lost ... for a short time. It turned up four days hence in the hot tub, deck 9. Apparently large ships do conserve and reprocess freshwater.

And if, between bites, one has any spare time, there are many activities aboard. Our ship had a tennis court, deck shuffleboard, two swimming pools, lounges with nightly entertainment, a ship's company theater group to put on nightly shows, and a casino.

Ahh, yes ... the casino. An interesting place while at sea. There one witnesses what I concluded was the ship's main engine room. Banks and banks of what are named *slot machines* gather cruise mates there around, who feed coins of various denominations thereinto, pull their main power handles, and the gears – decorated with bars, cherries, lemons, etc, to conceal their true meaning – spin 'round and 'round. And, the ship cruises on ... as did ours. Until, of course, it snuggled into a port of call. Then staff shoo-ed everyone out of the casino, pulled a metal gridwork wall across its entrance, and the great bar-cherry-lemon-etc. gears stopped. And, so did the great ship.

A day or so later, we re-crept out to sea. As soon as it was done, I examined again the casino. Surely as expected, the metal grid-work wall was pulled back, cruise mates again pulled the gear machines' main power handles, and the mighty decorated gears once again spun 'round and 'round. We cruised on.

After partaking of some twenty to thirty meals, and having picked clean the gift shop, my soul mate decided we needed to do our part to help propel the ship ... to pull our own weight, so to speak. So, in midafternoon, 'twas off to the casino with us.

We were now sailing lazily, between ports of call. There were not as many cruise mates tugging at the main power handles. This was not good. My beauty riffled through her purse, and I, my pockets. Four quarters. Four. That's all the ship fuel we could find on first examination. She directed me to approach a gear machine with main power handle and commence, and went to a "cashier's cage" to obtain more fuel.

The first quarter was deposited, the power handle pulled smartly and released. The mighty machine's gear wheels spun; spun ... and suddenly one came to an abrupt halt. Three cherries ... whatever that meant. Then in rapid succession did the second, and the last stop ... a lemon ... a bar. The machine yet thirsted.

A second coin of our four was offered thereto, the power handle manipulated as before, and the gear wheels spun on. Again they came to abrupt halts, from left to right, each displaying a different symbol: ... a lemon ... an orange ... a bar. But somehow, the machine did malfunction. A loud bell commenced its raucous clanging, perhaps a call for maintenance, and the gear machine spat out a few coins, evincing a malfunction, the coins falling into a large drip pan affixed to its lower front.

The bell clamored on. Coins continued dropping into the drip pan. I fished them out, held them, wondering whatever the matter was. But coins continued to dribble out. The great machine must have sprung a serious leak. As from the pan they were retrieved, it became increasingly difficult to hold all. I put them in my pockets, which shortly did decide to bulge considerably. Yet, coins fell to the pan.

The racket attracted attention from the few others powering the great boat forward. My wife, also curious, came to me, looked at the gearwheels, then at a large chart on the wall above. She said, "You hit it for two hundred quarters ... fifty dollars!"

She sported a straw handbag slung from her shoulder. We simply scooped the last of the coins into it, loosely. To lighten my awkward load, I emptied my pockets therein, as well. By and by the machine exhausted itself and went into a sulk. Its commotion stopped, the bell ceased to ring, its gear wheels remained still, and coins no longer dripped into the large pan. We retrieved the last of them.

Then, her beautiful, but excited voice intoned, "C'mon! Let's go!"

"Where?" I inquired.

To the gift shop, it seemed. "Quit while you're ahead!" the voice added.

It was then a light dawned, the realization set in that these machines were for gambling. I did protest: "No, you can't do that. This is gambling. I've been warned. It is but a pastime, entertainment. If you ever think you can gain by gambling, you become addicted to it, and that leads to ruin. The house always wins. We stay until we put all that, plus our budgeted amount, back into these hungry gear machines."

The sweet voice's counter – argument: "No problem. I can handle that. It doesn't happen often, and we aren't habitual gamblers." With that, she started for the exit. I grabbed the strap of that large straw bag, arrested her march. She turned to face me: "What!?"

My counter – counter: "It's only fifty bucks. I'd need to claim it as gambling winnings on our tax return, fill in extra forms, read more instructions. Taxes are complicated enough without that added headache." Her counter – counter – counter: "I'll fill out the forms."

The bell on the gear machine must have been modeled after Pavlov, for my love was so salivating about the expected gift shop visit. It was hard to resist. But again, as she turned toward the door, I tugged at that shoulder strap.

She spun around, exuded some frustrated anger, snapping, "Now what?"

My final rebuttal:

"Look at you. Five days sunning yourself poolside beneath the Caribbean sun, in a bikini offering just sufficient coverage to be legal … barely. And, if I do say so myself, and I do, you are a stunning example of womanhood, in spite of our eating ourselves silly this last week. Your feminine wiles, gorgeous curves, beautiful face, no man could resist if you but turned on your charm. I thank you for reserving it exclusively for me. However, in two days we will be back at the port of Miami."

The complimentary tone cooled her growing anger a tad. She knew how much I loved her. She felt my kiss and caress daily. Nightly , too. From her came, "So?"

I continued:

"This boat is of foreign registry. We'll need to go through customs."

Another "So?"

"As you approach the inspector, I'll dash around the corner, leave you alone."

"So?"

"Now, what do you think they will think? They see you, such a stunning creature, seemingly traveling alone, leaving a tour boat after one week with a bag full of quarters?"

A slight pause, then a seething look of daggers, then, "You (expletive)!"

We stayed. We put all those coins, plus our previously budgeted amount, back into the great gear machines. And thankfully, too. The great ship continued on its way, and we had done our part,

Mephisto

They were good years, the late 60s, for the two of them. They had been married for a while and were somewhat settled into life together, very comfortable with each other, not poor, not rich, but somewhere in the middle class. They had their first house, a wonderful pet dog, a car, a small boat, and deeply cherished the time they spent together. He had earlier earned a bachelor's degree in physics. She had pursued hers in chemistry.

He took employment at the university, in the chemistry department, a position whose perks included half-tuition at his choice of classes. He worked on his graduate degree.

On registering for his first semester, he found he lacked one credit to take two graduate courses. Each required four, while the perks granted only seven. The professor, his employer, inquired: Would he pay the one credit and take two courses? He could not, as their finances, with her enrolled in classes, just did not support it, nor did their schedule. He was an Army reservist and was required to spend every other weekend at the local armory with his unit.

The professor then said, "Well, it would be a shame to waste those three credits. Sign up for German ... it's only a three-credit course.

"German? Why?"

"Well, my boy," continued the professor, "prior to World War I, chemistry *was* German! And I can always use another translator in the department."

So, German it was. He took the first two semesters. She had previously done so, and they decided to study the language together for the next five semesters, husband and wife, lover and lovee, coeds, and found it a deeply rewarding way of spending quality time together.

About the third semester of German, one begins a study of its literature, and the university had a wonderful fine arts department, specializing in music and theatre, where the many literary works are interpreted and performed. So German lit, as it was called, was a very well organized and worthwhile course of study. They found many works fascinating – Three Penny Opera by Bert Brecht, the writings of Hermann Hesse, Max Frisch, others. One semester she presented an assigned extra study report on the opera Wozzeck, while his presentation was a radio play, Das Unternehmen der Wega. [9] And, by and by, they sank into more and more involved works, leading them through a two-semester study of Goethe's major work, *Faust*.

There are many Faust-like stories through the ages. The central theme: a man, dissatisfied with how things are, or his lack of understanding, is approached by the Devil, offered a means to quench that dissatisfaction in return for his soul upon his death. Several of these involve a twinge of trepidation on the part of the man, who negotiates a contractual "escape clause" that may be exercised at the man's option. One example of a Faust-like story is the movie *Damn Yankees*.

Goethe's Faust is a classic and, perhaps, the best known example of such a story. While a serious work of man's insatiable thirst for more than he has, the Devil, named Mephistopheles, plays the part of comic relief. As an example, Mephisto, as he is quickly nicknamed, becomes exasperated at Faust's continual demands, regrets ever having made the contract, and exclaims, "Why, I'd go to the Devil, were I not he in person!"

---

[9] *The Journey of the Vega*, a sci-fi story of a visit to Venus.

Owing to the strong drama and music components of the university's curriculum, there were several concomitant German classes each semester. Herr Professsor Doktor Genschmer, head of the modern languages department, was their favorite professor. An old-school, very straight-laced and strict instructor, he disdained poor work. One's grades reflected that deeply. But, for those who enjoyed the subject and studied it diligently, the opposite was true. As for most in the teaching field, the eager student who learns willingly is one of life's great rewards.

It was a symbiotic relationship. They thoroughly enjoyed the subject. They enjoyed study time spent together without outside annoyances and demands. They even continued through nightly pillow talk. Herr Professor maintained them as consistent A-B students.

In class, Herr Professor would, according to his style, ask a question of the students. Then he would consult his small black notebook, selecting one who had not recently been called upon for an answer. And, for one such question, they both knew the correct answer – Mephisto. Herr Professor scanned that little book, and called her name.

They were seated in the front row, alongside each other, their customary position. Without hesitation, she began her answer:

"Mef ...Meph ... Mmmme...."

Now, we've all had an episode where, because of dry mouth, tangled tongue, or something similar, we stammer a word that otherwise flows easily. And just then, she was so caught. Obviously, she knew the correct answer. Herr Professor waved both hands in encouragement, the gesture that says, "C'mon, c'mon ... spit it out." Her spouse did the same.

While she took a breath and wet her lips with a quick flip of the tongue, a voice from the back of the room chimed, "Hat der Teufel Ihre zunge?" This unexpected interruption caught the class off guard. It interrupted her answer. Her mental acuity turned to translation. And, as the translation – Devil got your tongue? – crept across the room, the awkward silence gave way to the humor of the situation.

But Herr Professor's class was not one in which joking was condoned. All sat there, each in turn as the translation occurred to them, trying hard to suppress the reaction to an outright belly laugh. The professor, too, was slowly distracted by the injected change of mood, drew himself upright, leaned back against his desk, and began a laugh, slowly at first, then much more heartfelt. Thusly, the room's tension was released, and all had a good laugh for half a minute.

Then, reacquiring his nominal strict composure, professor took his handkerchief, wiped his glasses, and in impeccable German announced what translates to, "If the author or authoress of that comment will make himself or herself known, he or she shall receive an **A** for originality ... and an **F** for conduct!"

Total silence followed.

Blazes

We lived at the end of a long lane, on a nice wooded lot, alongside a small stream. An electrical highline followed the lane from the road to a pole outside the house, on which a transformer massaged the voltage to house-size. I'm told the line was at about seven thousand volts.

Having achieved that status in life known as codgerhood, and concomitantly the state of rising about four A.M, I stepped out of bed, waking the family dog. She thought: He's off to mark his territory again. And, she was right.

Our bedroom faced the yard and pole. That mid-morning, half asleep, I witnessed from outside the window a sudden flash of lightning. Strange, I thought. The evening before had been rather starry, no cloud in the sky. Nor had the TV weather prophets offered such a prognosis. Quite the opposite.

While in the bathroom, I noticed another flash, and another shortly after. But came no thunder. The flashes were too intense to be heat lightning in the distance; they seemed to be rather close. Thereupon I pulled the shade aside, and beheld a few more flashes that began to occur closer and closer together, and finally became one continuous, brilliant, blue-white light, as if one were arc welding in the yard.

I rubbed my eyes, awakened further, and looked, wide eyed. And yes, a welder's arc was there, in the front yard; an intense light that illuminated the entire area by its harsh glow. It was a few tens of feet above the small creek in a tree. The latter, growing along the creek bank, had its root system eroded away considerably, had developed quite a "lean," and was now touching the high line. Yet, power to the house was still present.

The transformer in the yard fed only one residence – ours. I realized that, shortly, our electricity would fail, so I walked to the kitchen to use the phone, allowing my wife to continue her sound sleep.

The phone directory provided the correct number. I called the local electric utility's emergency line. A friendly computer instructed me that offices were closed, but directed me through a litany of button pushes to register my reason for calling:

"If this is an emergency push one."

I did so. It continued, "If your lights are out, push three. If your phone is not working, push four. If you do not understand English, push five. To hear these instructions in Swahili, push six. If there is an elephant stampede in your driveway, push seven."

Well, something like that. My sleepy, yet anxious state about the arc light in the yard kept me from accurately recalling the actual instructions. The list above is about as useful as what it did say. An emergency response seemed not plausible; whereupon I phoned the police dispatcher non-emergency line.

"County dispatch."

"Good morning. I have a small problem. A tree is leaning against the electric line leading to my property and is catching fire."

"Did you say fire?"

"Yes. The tree is catching fire."

"You can actually see fire?" "

Michael Toia

"Yes. Fire. Smoke. Falling embers. But it's no emergency. The whole thing can burn to the ground and it won't do anything other than burn itself out. I tried to call the electric company, but can't seem to get through. Can you call them for me?"

"Sir ... hang up immediately. Call 911 and report the fire."

Well, it didn't appear to be such an emergency at first, but now the tree was burning rather well at the arcing point, and purplish-red, electric, brush-like discharges began to streak upward a few inches from the tips of some branches. The leaves were burning off and falling into the creek or onto the grass. So I called 911, gave my name and address, and reported the situation.

The local fire station was several hundred feet along the road from my driveway. In less than a minute its siren wailed. An engine came forth, down the road, past my driveway, and off into the distance. In just two minutes it returned, again past the driveway, and off into the opposite distance. Again in a few minutes it returned, passed the driveway, and disappeared. I called 911 again.

"County dispatch."

"Are you trying to dispatch a fire engine to 1715 Winding Road?"

"Yes."

"Tell them they passed my driveway three times. It's between Jerry's Mower Repair shop and the very large oak tree ... a small gravel lane."

"Thank you. I'll direct them."

Without further ado the engine reappeared, turned down my driveway, and I met the crew out alongside the house. There, two hundred feet down the yard, was the tree, the arc light still dazzling, fire and smoke aplenty, embers falling to the ground, and many of the twig ends showing those purplish four-inch electric brush-like discharges. I told them I simply wanted to ask the electric company to come, turn off the power, remove the tree, and restore electricity to my home.

The firemen said they couldn't do anything about the fire since electricity was still on, but they did have a means to call the electric utility's emergency crew and did so. They said all they could do is leave one man on site to observe the fire and alert the others if it got out of control. It was five A.M. I said I was not going back to bed, but rather would sit on the porch and watch the fireworks. So, they told me to keep it in sight, let them know if it got dangerous, and took their leave.

Well! A show! And what a show it was. The whole tree lit up with those brush-like electric discharges from each and every one of its branchlets, no exceptions. The arc light continued, the fire slowly spread up the tree trunk, smoke intensified, and embers showered down into the creek. It was a display like none I had witnessed in my lifetime. I near felt a religious calling. Moses witnessed a burning bush. What a piker. I had a forty-foot tree throwing smoke, fire and embers, and discharging four-inch electric brushes skyward from all of its twiglets. It was enough to convert all but the most recalcitrant of atheists.

The show continued until six. Then, with a big POW! the arc light abruptly failed, lights went out, the house and yard fell again dark, the electric discharges disappeared. All that remained was the bit of fire on the tree trunk, some smoke, and falling embers, but this, too, subsided in about fifteen minutes.

I dozed off until sunrise about 7 A.M. At 7:30 a small truck from the electric utility company appeared. Its three-man crew mounted a pruning saw on their hot stick, and in ten minutes, had the top of the tree sawed away, free of the highline, then replaced the fuse at the road. Our power was restored.

It was a memorable night. I had had a considerable conversation with God through it all. It was truly awesome.

Michael Toia

Meg

A senior chemistry student working as a part-time student assistant, she had long, brown hair usually worn up, was not particularly attractive, with a rather normal-looking face. She worked in the main central chemistry lab, and almost always was off near one corner, standing and working at a bench, or sitting on a tall lab stool conducting or observing the progress of her work.

The laboratory contained, perhaps, one of the largest gas transport lines in the department. These are grids of aluminum rods, at about 6" intervals, horizontal and vertical, floor to ceiling, on which were mounted many feet of glass tubing, flasks, condensers, water lines, vacuum manifolds, and all sorts of usually Pyrex chemistry apparatus of myriad sorts. Mechanical pumps sat on the floor, constantly intoning a ubiquitous, "Blurp, blurp, blurp, blurp, blurp," as they maintained the fore pump manifold vacuum.

Oil diffusion pumps made of Pyrex, mounted on the gridwork, constantly sucked away at the high vacuum main manifold that ran the length of the apparatus, delivering their output to the fore pump manifold. Cryogenic "cold traps" sat here and there, emitting the steam-like vapor of cold gas boiling away from the liquid nitrogen inside. The whole was a neo-fiction looking "mad scientist" setup. But it was real, very real ... part of research in organic chemistry.

This large, general-purpose setup occupied the center of the laboratory. Entrance and egress was to the main hallway running down the centerline of the second floor. The hallway did a sequence of four right angle turns to carry foot traffic around the large laboratory area. Students and faculty alike avoided the lab both out of a sense of foreboding fear, and so as not to disturb the progress therein.

However, department staff knew that they could take a shortcut through it, to transit from one end of the hall to that at the other, but infrequently did so.

Now to Meg, off in one corner of the lab. She was on the slightly tall side of average, and as said a rather average looking young lady in some respects, but not all. She was, well, well-endowed in the chest area, very well indeed. I never took calipers or tape measure to her, but no one needed to. Her upper chest was obviously her most pronounced and attractive asset, one any woman could desire. And, she wore the tightest fitting blouses and sweaters that set off those assets in the most positive and dramatic way.

She had a rather trim waist, and complementary long, shapely legs. Accentuating the sweater or blouse, she wore the tightest fitting slacks that possibly could contain her curves. If one entered the lab, and one were male, age fifteen to a hundred, a glance or look at Meg was impossible to avoid. One needed to navigate carefully, to work one's way around the giant gas transport line. All the staff that used the shortcut was aware of the jogs needed in the trans-laboratory shortcut, and their auto-response guidance system kept them on the proper path.

Came a day when a new staff member hired on. He was a really good, upcoming chemist, getting the hang of our building's labs and setup, and how to navigate about. And one day he happened to be walking down the hall from the rear to the front of the building, and recalled that someone mentioned a shortcut through the large central lab, and in passing had mentioned Meg. So, our subject, on approaching the lab, finding its door open, strolled inside, and began looking about to pick his way through the shortcut.

Michael Toia

And it happened. As he glanced about, he spotted Meg, sitting on a lab stool, doing her work. His attention to detail took a strong turn to the matter, but his automatic motor functions kept moving his body straight ahead at normal speed. He collided with that main line. The sound could be heard well outside the lab, as large quantities of Pyrex tubing, flasks, and assorted glass components, all under high vacuum, imploded, glass shards flying off in all directions. Fortunately he was not badly injured, needing only a handful of band-aids to patch his body and stem the light flow of blood.

Routinely, I brown-bagged lunch with Ray, a good friend, the chief of chemical stores. His office and crew had responsibility for overall cleanliness and supply of all labs. The vacuum line mess cleanup was his to handle. He told me the story, as well as he knew it. I had myself caught glimpses of Meg, but not being a chemist, avoided the shortcut through the lab. I knew it to be dangerous, so did not tempt fate.

Ray said, "What am I to do? You've seen Meg. It's impossible not to catch a glance of her; men are just primal creatures in that regard. But look at what happened! And I've had informal complaints that this was likely inevitable. I've discussed it in weekly department meetings. But we can't fire her. She does good work and it's not her fault God gave her those curves. I wish I knew what to do."

I half-jokingly said, "Put an A-frame caution placard on the floor at both entrances to the lab, saying "CAUTION: EYE HAZARD AREA."

Later that afternoon, as I transited the main hall, there they were, at each end of the lab. Ray and I both knew the origin of their placement. Several of the staff either heard from Ray, his staff, or else figured it out on their own. It was basically a 'no-brainer.' I know not if Meg ever was told, or figured it out on her own. We often mused about it.

Radioactive

The university employed a nucleonic engineer, to tend the electronic apparatus that supports research on radioactive material. The position afforded half-time tuition, and provided the means by which I obtained a masters degree in physics, though employed by the Department of Chemistry in the field of Nuclear Chemistry, the realm of radio chemists. These folk use radioactive materials in chemistry to do quantitative analysis. The more radioactivity, the more of a radioactive atom in the measured sample. A good example of this is what is called radiocarbon dating. When vegetation lives, it takes on carbon dioxide from the atmosphere and sequesters it in the carbon-containing cellulose of the plant's woody structure. When the plant dies, the absorption of carbon dioxide ceases.

Now carbon dioxide is a component of the atmosphere. Most of it contains carbon-12, each atom containing six protons and six neutrons. But a tiny fraction of natural carbon dioxide contains carbon-14, with not six, but eight neutrons per atom. Carbon 14 is radioactive. Carbon 12 is not.

The ratio of the two in atmospheric carbon dioxide is essentially constant, and many measurements confirm this constant has not changed in thousands of years. So, if an unknown sample of wood or cellulosic material is processed and its carbon extracted, one may simply determine how radioactive the sample is. The less radioactive, the older the sample, for its initially radioactive carbon-14 dies away exponentially, leaving less behind.

I was proud to have worked on a methane proportional counter, a large steel tube filled with methane gas, a tiny bit of which our radio chemists had synthesized from a few milligrams of Dead Sea scroll material. Our lab agreed with scores of others, that the sample did, indeed, date from old-testament biblical times.

At any one time there were between twenty and twenty-four separate nuclear detector systems in our research area. My function was to run routine calibrations on these, do maintenance as need be, modify or design and build selected systems to perform additional experiments, and so forth. We had alpha detectors and spectrometers, beta detectors, gamma detectors and spectrometers, and some other specialized, assorted measurement systems.

One day I met a chap from electrical engineering in the cafeteria. He asked if chemistry could determine the percentage of gold doping in a semiconductor, down to a few parts per million, with at least 10 percent accuracy. I said I would check with my colleagues and get back to him, and later broached the subject with one of the staff radio chemists.

When the subject of gold in a semiconductor was thrashed about, my colleague consulted his books and tables, furrowed his brow a bit, and said it would likely be difficult to get that sort of accuracy. That is, until he said, "… parts per million! I thought you said billions! My gosh, yes; we can tell down to fractions of a percent."

The procedure is called Neutron Activation Analysis. One takes a pedigreed sample of some substance whose chemistry is well known, and that contains very little or accurately known amounts of radioactivity. This and the substance to be tested are packed together, sent to a nuclear reactor facility, and are placed in a thermal neutron port for some period of time. In both samples, the atoms absorb neutrons and transmute to isotopes next to them in the periodic table. The new isotopes are radioactive and begin to decay away, producing very well known beta and / or gamma rays, which reduce in intensity exponentially with the characteristic half-life of the particular isotopes. The intensity of this radiation is directly proportional to the amount of original atoms present.

The pedigreed sample is a flux monitor. Measuring it certifies the total neutron flux that had irradiated the package. Then the substance to be tested is examined, and separating the radioactivity from, say, radiation products of germanium and gold allow one to determine the ratio of gold to germanium in it.

We met with the electrical engineers. We visited their labs. We saw beakers, test tubes, bottles and jars of J. T. Baker & Co. chemicals, and everything that a good chemistry lab ought to have. They visited our lab. They saw stacks and rows of electronic equipment, blinking lights, voltmeters, oscilloscopes, electronic test and measurement equipment.

Good Lord! The two disciplines had exchanged labs and technology!

In rather short order their request was satisfied by our staff. We had been very happy to provide the analytic services.

Now it happened that we sent materials out for neutron irradiation quite frequently. We did not have a nearby reactor, so shipped our samples by air freight several hundred miles off to a reactor facility with an order indicating how long they should be steeped in the thermal neutron flux. Once they were so treated, the new radioactive materials began to die off with their characteristic half-life, in many cases much less than a day. It was imperative to get the sample back as quickly as possible. The reactor lab shipped them by express air freight, phoned us and gave us the flight number and schedule. The radio chemist working on that sample would drive to the airport, meet that flight, retrieve his sample shipment, and return to the lab as quickly as possible, to begin analysis with minimum delay.

One Friday Ray, a post-doctorate research fellow, met the scheduled flight at 10 A.M. His shipment was not on board, but the reactor lab had assured him it was. So Ray consulted with the air shipment company, who indicated it would be on the next flight due in early afternoon. Hmmm. One half-life gone … the sample would be only half as hot as before.

The sample was not on the next fight, nor the next, nor any that Friday or Saturday. Ray, of course, slept not during this time; yet still had a lot of chemical analysis to do once the sample should arrive. By Sunday noon it was obvious that the experimental analysis would be impossible. Ray retired to his home and got a bit of fitful sleep.

Monday morning the air freight company called. His package was on the loading dock at the airport. Ray came to my lab. He asked, "You have portable Geiger counters?" Of course, I did. Ray asked if I could mis-calibrate one so it fried like a house afire with just normal everyday background radiation. I did so. Then he said, "Perfect! Come with me."

"Where to?" Well, we got in his car, went to the airport, to the air freight company, and were led to their loading dock. There it was, a roughly half-cubic foot small, tough, wooden box, lead lined, with "Caution – Radioactive" labels on all its surfaces. Ray approached it, then turned the Geiger counter ON, waving its wand about. It fried like no tomorrow. He backed off, said, "Wow! That's a bit too hot to handle right now. Let it cool off a bit; we'll be back Friday."

We went back Friday with the Geiger counter properly re-calibrated. There was the little box, waaaaaay off in the corner, all by its lonesome, with yellow caution tape all around it. The Geiger counter now sounded more normal, so we took the package, signed for it, and drove back to campus.

Our shipments after that always seemed to come through very expeditiously. It just takes a little nudging to get union workers to want to do the job, I guess.

Michael Toia

Toast

Roy, a graduate student in chemistry, was a colleague, a close friend, and I, an instrumentation engineer in charge of equipment design, selection, and maintenance. We worked together closely for several years.

The chemistry labs were not posh. Quite the opposite. Roy's had the usual stone-top long table with sink, and a large cross-hatched, floor-to-ceiling aluminum frame supporting all sorts of glass tubing, flasks, high vacuum valves, and myriad paraphernalia to work with chemicals in the vapor state. Vacuum pumps occupied the floor behind, and a large U-tube, mercury-filled manometer adorned its right side. Racks of electronic measuring equipment occupied more floor space to the right.

Office buildings have a finished drop ceiling, a grid of 2' x 4' ceiling tiles, fluorescent lights, and ventilators. Roy's lab had none of that. Light fixtures hung about two feet below the slab floor of the room above, and dimly above those could be seen pipes, plumbing, electrical conduit, and so forth.

A few windows adorned the one wall behind the chemical table. They were kept open, wider in summer and just an inch or so in winter. Mercury spills from that open-top manometer would sometimes occur, and chemists then were well aware of the effects of mercury vapor poisoning. Fresh air ventilation was a necessity.

A small desk sat in a corner, crammed amongst all the other equipment and material. A bookcase sat alongside, and a small one rested on the rear of the desk. A goose-neck desk lamp supplemented the room's otherwise inadequate light. Roy completed several years of graduate work in this environment.

Occasionally some splotches of whitewash-looking material would appear on his desk. He would clean it up, but the source was puzzling. By and by we discovered it, There was a pigeon's nest in the gloom, in the maze of plumbing and piping above the desk!

Now, how did that get there? And, it contained a few eggs! Whose idea of a practical joke was this? Yes, the all-too-frequent joke provided well-needed lubricant for the skids of life's stresses. Someone had built a nest of hay-like material, placed it above Roy's desk, put some fake eggs into it, and occasionally splashed whitewash droplets on the desk as imitation pigeon poo. What a lot of effort … and this continued for months. The prankster was tenacious.

The fake nest was realistic in all details … very realistic. It even attracted a pigeon. One day Roy saw a pigeon fluttering down from the nest toward the open window, and squeeze between the bottom of the sash and sill. It flew off. AHA! The nest was *real*. A mother pigeon found it a cozy spot, a refuge from wind, rain, snow, and cold. She found Roy's open window as a way inside, the nest of plumbing up in the corner, and made it her home. We knew a colony of pigeons maintained a collective loft nearby, up under the giant overhang of the old building, but mother preferred this as her home.

Roy closed the window. In a while mother was back, unable to get in to her nest. She began beating on the window with her wings, pecking at it with her beak, raising considerable commotion. Roy wanted to concentrate on his studies. Mother made this impossible. Roy opened the window just a crack, and began thrashing at mother's feet with a handy laboratory meter stick. Roy thrashed. Mother danced, but continued her frantic commotion. Peace was not to be had.

Roy then took a one-liter "wash bottle," a plastic bottle with a long tube running down inside and exiting so the contents could be squirted out, filled it with acetone from his chemical bench, and began spraying mother, expecting she would find the chemical odor and strong cooling effect bad enough to give up her quest. The ruse failed. Mother prevailed.

Roy lit a Bunsen burner and tried to toast mother's feet. But she was a bit soaked in acetone, and burst into flames! That did it. Mother took flight, left the window sill, swooped in a big flaming arc down across the campus mall, circled back, and took refuge in the main pigeon loft. It caught fire!

The fire department was summoned, responded, and shortly had all under control. Carpenters and painters then took over for a week or so and repaired the damage. At least Roy and mother came to a peaceful understanding: she would stay out of Roy's lab.

Steamed

Father once worked for Alcoa, the large aluminum firm. He was a master machinist, tool and die maker, and instrument maker. He was part of a small development team, investigating various products that might be produced from aluminum. I recall one that he related to me – the aluminum beer keg. So my family, through father, was indeed a great benefactor of mankind, let no man deny.

Many aluminum products were developed and sent out to test market. Aluminum cafeteria trays were one. But, when certain foods spilled onto them, they developed a permanent stain. Investigation of these led to discovery of a process known as anodizing, whereby the aluminum was electrochemically treated, leaving on its surface a hard, protective oxidized coating whose color could be varied to a rainbow of brights. It led to considerable application in both the industrial and consumer markets.

Cookware was a natural extension of the development. Aluminum is lighter than iron, conducts heat better, and is today used in a variety of pots, pans, skillets, and so forth.

In the invention of cookware, along came a pressure cooker, a closed vessel that would contain the steam of boiling water under pressure. As steam pressure increases, so does its temperature. Therefore the pressure cookers would subject food to higher temperature than would an open pot, and the food would cook in less time. The pressurized steam also penetrates the food product more easily and assists in softening items such as dried beans and peas, potatoes, carrots, and so forth. This considerably shortens the cooking process.

Early pressure cookers had a tight-fitting lid with a gasket to prevent steam escape, and a pressure gauge. The cook had to pay attention to the gauge lest the pressure build up to dangerous levels and the cooker rupture, with a steam explosion of considerable force and high temperature. Early devices were somewhat dangerous. Most, if not all, were fitted with a safety blow-out plug, much like an electrical fuse, that would pop and vent steam in a safe direction if the internal pressure became too high.

Alcoa developed a nice little pressure cooker, with a capacity of a few quarts. It was a fairly deep pot, and had a flexible lid that fit inside the pot, then flexed to close the top against a gasket inside the pot. The center of the lid had a small stem, a little pipe, out of which steam could escape. It also had a rubber safety plug as a backup. Should steam pressure become dangerous, the plug would just blow out and vent steam in a safe direction, toward the ceiling.

On the pipe sat a small weight. This would prevent steam from escaping until the pressure reached a designated value. Then the weight would lift a bit, let steam escape, and would loosely 'jiggle' atop the pot while cooking continued.

Well, mother became one of the original pre-market testers of this little gem. Father brought one home. Mom liked new gadgets and was delighted with this one. She tried cooking various foods, using the Alcoa kitchen's test recipes' recommendations. Father would take her comments back to the test kitchens for compilation.

I, a rather young boy of ten, benefited considerably from the testing. We were rather simple folk, lived on a not very extravagant budget, and consumed a good share of beans, potatoes, and very little, if any, steak. Pot roast or stew was a delicacy.

Michael Toia

One day mom tried a recipe for chili. This started with dried beans. Open pot cooking required that the beans be soaked in salted water overnight. The pressure cooker did not need this step, and considerably lessened the cooking time.

By this time, mom was used to the fact that the little jiggling pressure-regulating weight needed heeding. If it stopped its happy little "psst ... psst ... psst" for more than a minute, you needed to tap it with a spoon or something to get it going again. Bits of food would sometimes work through the little vent pipe and get lodged against the jiggling weight.

That day, the jiggler stopped for a while. Mom tapped it. No reaction. She tapped it again. Still no dice. The third time was the charm. The thing shot off the top of the cooker, propelled violently on a menacing column of very loud hissing of steam.

I was in the living room, sprawled on the floor doing my homework. The sound of that thing, the roaring hiss of steam, scared the bejeebers out of me! I shot to my feet, made for the living room door opposite the kitchen, into the hallway, and down the stairs from our second-floor apartment, to exit stage front just as rapidly as my adrenaline-infused legs could carry me.

Mom passed me partway down.

Salt

There are many stories yet to be told. I relate here one that gathers various dots in history, mentally connected to propose the following sequence, a story of how European influx to the New World led inexorably to the development of an airplane capable of powered flight, and on to jet aircraft.

Throughout the 1800s, immigration saw European peoples come to North America, slowly at first, but in gradually increasing numbers. They landed by ship at the Atlantic Coast and seeped, spread inland, Westward bound, and pressed against the Alleghenies, that mountain range stretching NE-SW from Maine to Georgia, roughly paralleling the eastern coast.

The Alleghenies presented a bit of a barrier to Westward expansion. They were difficult to cross with wagon trains of provisions, tools, and items of life's necessities and comfort. Of these, a small collection of tools, minimal provisions, and practically no comfort paraphernalia were dragged up the mountains, through the wind gaps, and down the other side onto the Western foothills to the navigable waters of the Western river system, most leading to the Ohio and the Mississippi. At the headwaters of these rivers, the Westbound pioneers could take to river boats or something similar and continue inland to colonize the Great Plains up onto the eastern foothills of the Rockies. However, re-provisioning was needed.

Industries grew where mountain trails met the rivers. Farms provided food. This was processed, preserved, and packed for transportation and later consumption. Refrigeration was a century or so into the future. Brine packaging was exceedingly common – salt pork, brine pickles, many foodstuffs packed in salt. Bacteria cannot grow in heavily saline baths, and the salt itself was consumable by humans with little ill effect, or could be leached out of the food with fresh water. Hence, there developed a large industry devoted to salt production.

Now, how do the Western Alleghenies produce salt? Their streams are fresh water. Evaporation pans, such as those common on the West Coast and elsewhere, would not do. But, there was a way.

Fresh drinking water is oft drawn from wells. These may be just a few feet deep to a hundred or more. Many a home, yet today, is provided water from wells. Deeper wells often produce less contaminated and better-tasting water. I know not how it came about, but wells drilled many hundreds of feet beneath the surface were found to produce brine – salt water – water with salinity much stronger than the oceans. So, deep wells were drilled down into the earth, brine pumped to the surface, and run off into large settling ponds where it could evaporate and yield the desired salt.

There was a problem with this salt. It tasted awful. A contaminant came up with the brine ... rock oil ... petroleum ... Texas tea. This stuff floated on the brine, so the ponds were skimmed to remove the contaminant, which was then simply poured down the creeks and streams, polluting surface waters.

A small industry grew up about the rock oil. It was bottled and taken westward, and sold as a remedy for assorted and myriad ills. Historically it was called variously rock oil, or more euphemistically, snake oil. As with most medicinal products of the time, it tasted just awful, had a disgusting texture to it. Thus, it had to be useful for medicinal purposes. 'Tis said more than one person recovered from its use, generally to avoid the need of repeated dosage.

Rock oil had another disagreeable property. If the skimmers smoked a pipe while performing their chore, the pond sometimes blew up. The oil had lighter naphtha oil fractions that were quite flammable and evaporated readily, yielding a heavier-than-air vapor along the surface of the pond. Today we call it gasoline.

About the middle of the nineteenth century, an oil shortage occurred. More and more homes and cabins were being built, and these wanted for light – oil lamps. The oil industry had trouble keeping up. There were just insufficient whales to be harvested for their oil. The rock oil, that unpleasant by-product of salt production, could not directly be burned as a substitute lamp oil. It stank. It had the wrong consistency. It readily caught fire, too, and was a bit of an explosion hazard.

Along came an enterprising young man, one of the Kier family sons. The Kiers owned oil fields north of Pittsburgh, and well into the 1960s. I know of one such field with five wells that still pumped Pennsylvania crude, one in particular known as Kier No. 5, east of Verona, PA, my hometown at the time.

The Kier son found a way to distill the crude rock oil, and extract various fractions from it. One was kerosene. He developed a modified oil lamp that could satisfactorily burn this product. The kerosene and its burnt product both had a light odor, not unduly objectionable. And, hence, the oil industry was ignited, so to speak. The site of Kier's first still is commemorated with a historic marker along Wood Street in downtown Pittsburgh.

Now this produced a then-undesirable by-product – gasoline. There was little market for it. It was sold for pennies a gallon, and the excess production was simply poured down the sewers, leading to several occasional sewer explosions, and the rivers catching fire as the floating gasoline found a favorable wind and a flame. The material was simply too volatile and combustible.

At the time, the prime mover of factories, paddlewheel steamers, farm implements, locomotives, and the new electric dynamos was the steam engine. It burned fuel in a boiler, then admitted the heated steam into a piston / cylinder unit, which developed mechanical power. Though these machines were powerful, they were heavy. Their specific power – kilowatts per kilogram of mass – was too low for aviation use. They could not lift *themselves* off the ground, much less the rest of the airplane and any cargo.

Engineers came to understand that it wasn't the steam that did the work, but rather its heat. Hot air would do as well. So, they tried filling a cylinder full of air, with a bit of combustible fuel vapor inside, compressing the air, then setting fire to the mixture. Voila! The explosion heated the air, and the heat did the job of pushing the piston down and driving the rest of the engine. And they said, "Look, Ma … no boiler!" The internal combustion engine was born. Here was a motor with a much higher specific power. So, what to use for fuel?

History holds that Henry Ford envisioned the use of grain alcohol for his early model automobiles. However, gasoline was so plentiful, troublesome, and relatively volatile that history led to its use instead. This engine produced heat immediately in its power cylinder with no need of an external heavy boiler. It had a much higher specific power than its forerunners.

And, armed with the new internal combustion, gasoline-powered engine, the Wright brothers were able to launch their powered glider, fly it about, with the all-important final property differentiating gliders from modern aircraft – the ability to return at will to their starting point under their own power. Thus, the quest to go West, the quest for salt, led in a sequence of needs and inconveniences to the development of the gasoline engine, and true powered flight by aircraft that can fly back home at the end of their exploration.

Engineers continued their understanding of heat engines. They found other means besides pistons and cylinders to pass heat through an engine and extract therefrom mechanical power. The gas turbine engine is one such advancement, and the modern jet aircraft turbine engine does just that – using as a fuel, a material substantially that of kerosene.

The Block

My boyhood home in Southwestern Pennsylvania had a rich populace of European first- and second-generation Americans, my father being an Italian-American of the former category. As the countryside is hilly, the Italian contingent seemed to prefer houses on the steep hillsides, and ours was one such. The front entrance at street level opened directly to the living room, and the kitchen floor at the rear was some 20 feet or so above grade. The house was solidly built in the 1920s, with a reinforced concrete floor over a basement, and concrete block for the outside – large, double-sized concrete block.

Mother decided she would like a ventilation fan for her kitchen. Father considered the project, and one day began work. On a ladder some distance above ground, he removed mortar from about one of the large exterior concrete blocks. He drilled through to the interior wall to mark the place in the kitchen where the ventilation duct would be placed. As he was a meticulous man, his calculations placed the vent opening exactly where he had planned.

After working for some time to remove all the mortar surrounding the block, he slowly worried it out of place and into his arms, all the while on the ladder. Carefully, he descended, cradling the block in his arms, and returned to ground level.

Father then carried the block upslope to street level, entered the front door, and continued up the stairs to the second floor hallway and to the bathroom. A bit later, he reappeared in the living room, block in arms, and proceeded to the top of the cellar stairs. Mother looked out from the kitchen and asked, "What are you doing?"

Now father was admittedly the smartest man in the extended set of family members, and mother was known as one of the area's best cooks. Everyone readily admitted that father's I.Q. was the highest in the family. So, the exchange struck all as worthy of note.

Father replied, "I just removed this block from the kitchen wall to prepare installation of your ventilation fan. It seems so heavy. I carried it up to the bathroom scale. The darned thing weighs 52 pounds! Now I'm taking it to the basement where I'll store it."

Mother asked: "Why didn't you just bring the bathroom scale down to the block? It isn't as heavy and that might have been a lot easier."

Father:

- - - ! - - -

Yes, a tad of thought can sometimes make a job easier. And no one of us knows as much as all of us. Chalk one up for Mother.

Love ya, Mom. And you, too, Dad.

Red

The job once required frequent commuting between Washington and Chicago. I would find myself in a hotel room for several nights two or three times a month.

Though Chicago is a vibrant and interesting town, I missed my sweetheart during each and every visit. Nevertheless, the commuting eventually panned out, with a promotion and transfer to the city. We moved there, and enjoyed a few really nice years. However, this story is about that frequent air travel and an event a bit before the move.

My bride was, and is yet, a sweet, meek, unpretentious, beautiful woman. She has always been insecure, self-conscious, and thought herself below par in the category of what one calls "sexy." I guess the glamour girl era of the 40s and 50s had burned its impression into her very fiber, but that's a view I never saw. When we met, it was to me "love at first sight" and led to our wedding after an engagement of just a few months.

Her feeling of inferiority and lack of self-confidence was a bit troublesome. Time and again she would become a tad paranoid, thinking another woman could entice me and split us apart. Now, perhaps I should have felt flattered by that, but found it irksome, as

SHE was, and remains, the one and only woman in my life. To me, it is a simple matter of "till death us do part."

On each and every of my return trips, her beautiful face, her warm embrace, her sweet, soft voice greeted me. I was as a king!

Now came a time when we Washington-bound travelers departed the aircraft to enter the terminal. I sought that sweet, amazing face amongst the crowd. Not seeing it immediately was cause for concern. My honey had always caught my attention in a crowd when within a hundred paces or more, and every sighting of her from a distance casts me into love all over again. Was she there? Was she in an accident? Is she okay?

There was another in the waiting crowd that caught the eye of *everyone* in the terminal. It was a stunning, redheaded young lady, with amazing red hair, in a "hot pants" suit of matching color with little white polka dots, a fashion stylish for a year or so. This vision was impossible to ignore. As I cast my glance about, looking for my sweetheart, and not finding her, my gaze kept passing back and forth to the redhead.

My darling would be hurt if she saw me ogling another woman, and in particular, Red, beyond any doubt the most stunning female in the terminal that day, and quite likely the entire year. I truly love my wife, and want never to hurt her. Trying to avoid looking at Red and continuing into the waiting crowd, still not spotting my one-and-only, my path came close to Red, and passed her by. But, where was my sweetheart?

What was wrong? I was really beginning to worry.

Then that soft, familiar, and most comforting voice called my name. It came from behind me. How could my walk have passed the woman whom I could spot from afar in any crowd? My mind said, not possible. Could Red have been such a distraction? I don't think so.

I turned, yet saw my wife not. Again I heard her voice. There was Red. Was my honey just behind her? Where in the world was she?

Then Red spoke. She called my name, made eye contact and smiled in an amazing way that cannot be described. She approached and reached out to me! Who the heck is this woman? Did my sweetheart somehow send her to meet me? Why?

Red spoke again. Good grief! It *was* my heartthrob! Stunning! She had dyed her hair red, bought this then-trendy, amazing hot pants suit, and there she stood, the most beautiful and sexy female in the terminal, taking my arm, and off we went to baggage claim.

There are some events in life one does not forget. Had there been a camera handy, that vision I called Red that day could be shared with you. However, her image is stuck in my brain – indelible, fascinating, and tantalizing – to this day. Were I R2D2, I could throw out a holographic image for you to see. But, you will just need to take my word for it.

I still love ya, Red, after all these years. Thanks for being my life mate.

Ulf

Hired by the same firm in the same year, neither had met before. But shortly into our new employment, we did. His name strongly suggesting a German origin, I stretched the limits of a potential friendship: "Ulf? Polynesian origin, I presume?"

He just smiled, pulled himself to a very formal erect standing position, and replied, "No. I am proud Austrian. Do not confuse me as one of those Chermans." And, thus, began a warm, wonderful relationship of many a year.

I learned much from Ulf. He worked on one project and I another, and the project mix shifted over the years. The project lead requested my assistance from time to time, and supposedly value was added by my inputs. I never quite knew, as the projects were always under some sort of classified wrappings, such as being company proprietary, or reports to some government or industry system. Full disclosure of all details was withheld.

Through this, the friendship with Ulf grew. He was, in fact, a knowledgeable type, friendly, courteous, professional, yet had a delightful humorous bent to his manner. Everyone grew to know him, and to really like the man.

After several years I, too, was brought into the project area, and quite happily was assigned to share an office with Ulf. We got along wonderfully well. He and I were staff members on a crew working for a manager who was himself quite expert in the field, yet very fastidious. It was said that, at the end of a day, he would line things up on his desk, a pen and pencil lying flat, parallel to and near the front edge, pointing precisely to the left. If, for some reason, someone accidentally moved these, he would notice the next day. He was not overly demanding, but did require professionalism in his department. Ulf nicknamed him, "Bdolph." Why? Well, it was explained, "Adolph had already been used."

Ulf had an uncanny ability as a software user-breaker. We would get upgraded software packages. They would be disseminated onto our desk computers. He would be the first to have something go haywire in these. Bdolph would become exasperated. But in relatively short order, it would be found that Ulf was simply the first to stumble across some software 'bug' that the rest of us would eventually trip over. He was just that kind of a person.

An election year came up. I was chair at our local precinct, and spent a lot of time placing, then removing, those "lollipop" roadside and yard signs, VOTE FOR JOE DOE, etc. I obtained a good one, and modified it. On a bright Monday morning, before staff began to arrive, I posted it at the entrance to our industrial campus: ULF FOR SENATE, and was caught red-handed in the middle of the act by the company VP as he drove in from the main road. Oh gosh! Am I in trouble? However, he slowed quite a bit, with his window rolled down, and shouted, "Good job, Mike!" All I could do was stammer, "Th-thank you, sir."

And, at lunch, the sign was gone – it appeared instead at the entrance to the company cafeteria. That's how well liked Ulf was. Sort of one of a kind. To this day, I hold our friendship in warm regard.

Some of the staff, including the two of us, would take a longer coffee break at two in the afternoon. We used those to exchange ideas and approaches to the project. Several were rather conservative persons, and some, NRA members. One chap with a good liberal bent would come to the table, and oft announce his presence with, "And, what is the militia up to today?" At one of these, I inquired as to his age. He was over eighteen, yet under fifty-six. It gave me a bit of pleasure to inform him that, according to state code, a state resident in that age range, including himself, was a member of the state militia-at-large, though I was over age and no longer a member. He was not happy to receive this news. I very cheerfully mentioned in passing that I sleep with a militia member: my wife was still in the proper age group. Thereafter, his greeting on approach to our group changed.

Now it happened that one member of our break group, a chap from an Asian country, approached with quite a puzzled look on his face. He brought along an official-looking letter he had received, bearing the White House seal: "Greetings from the President of the United States." It was a draft notice. Of course, by that time, no one had been drafted for many years. It was quite obviously some sort of a joke, and likely one he was hatching upon us. We simply went along with it.

He played the dummy, asked what this was, what it meant, employing his best and quite convincing acting abilities. We told him it meant he had thirty days to put his affairs in order, then he must report for active duty in the Army. This little game went on for several afternoon coffee breaks, he playing the convincing part of a deeply concerned person, we going along with the whole charade.

Well, he was *not* playing dumb, but as a recently naturalized citizen, was in fact not aware of the passing of the draft. He took the whole matter seriously. In due time, as he approached management saying he had to leave the employ of the company, he learned that it was a joke, perhaps a rather cruel one at that. And then, as is said, "it hit the fan – The wind blew, the poo flew, we couldn't see for a day or two." Management became concerned that, having spent thousands of dollars to recruit each and every good employee, they were about to lose one.

Time had passed. The poor subject of the joke was ready to quit, and did so. I'm told he went back to his home country, taking a very bad taste of America with him. In addition, he must have filed a complaint, for management conducted an investigation into the circumstances of the situation.

And lo! It came back to Ulf. Apparently, it was he who had concocted the whole thing – obtained an old draft notice, copied it, photoshopped it, made a very good facsimile of the real thing, added the intended victim's name, and mailed it to him. I found this from chats with Ulf. He related that the company vice president had, after some investigation, called him into his office, the fake draft notice prominently laid upon his desk, and asked, "Ulf … did you have anything to do with this?" as he pointed to the notice.

And Ulf, as he told me, stood there in a military style we would call as "standing at strict attention" and said, "Sir, I cannot deny it."

With that, the vice president said this had gone too far, a reprimand was in order, and Ulf need take this day's verbal exchange as that reprimand, and needed to take more care with what starts as a seemingly harmless joke that gets totally out of hand. Then, approaching Ulf, I am told he patted him firmly on the back, broke into a broad smile, and said,

"But, it's the best darned practical joke I've ever seen!"

Michael Toia

Dumdum's

The draft was yet a fact in the early sixties, pulling young men by lottery into the armed forces. One could be deferred if in college, but the sword of Damocles, waiting, suspended overhead by a single tiny thread, waiting to fall, was a haunt. To remove it, some signed up for Reserve Officers' Training Corps in college, and took a commission in the Armed Forces upon graduation. As one such ROTC graduate, I joined a line unit in 1961, a new lieutenant, and completed two years' service to my country.

The Army of the time was not coed. Some small units of WACS, the Women's Army Corps, existed. Work, play, and barracks accommodations were stringently separate by gender. The Army was one of men.

Promotion from second to first lieutenant, following eighteen months of honorable and satisfactory service, was practically automatic. It came to pass that four fellow lieutenants were so advanced. We held a small party in their honor, a gathering of a few battalion officers, about a dozen. As the shindig proceeded, we found our way to a small off-post bar, DUMDUM's, not fancy, but having a decent pub-type atmosphere and good beer. I do not like beer, but enjoyed the ambiance, camaraderie, and downed a reasonable amount of Coca-Cola.

Dumdum's sat in the Southeast of the US, in agricultural country, where it occupied a small building on a gentle hillside. A large rectangular room held the main bar and several tables in the front, narrowed halfway back to accommodate a side entrance outside of which hung a long set of stairs running parallel to the building, down to a parking lot at the rear. A small pool table prominently occupied the rear area, the capacity of which was insufficient to contain one of regulation-size, this being a Nine-Ball. I had never before seen one.

Young and still a bit inexperienced, I was mentored in pool by one Warrant Officer Landi. We saw the table, idle, inviting, and he introduced me to the game of Nine Ball. As my education proceeded, a few of the locals observed, three rather large, strapping young men noticeable in the group. By and by they engaged in conversation, then suggested we play for money.

Not that inexperienced, I recognized the standard 'hustle' maneuver at once, saw that the two of us may be headed to a tad bit of trouble, all the more so as my 5'11", 200-pound frame was smaller than any of the three, yet considerably more pronounced than my mentor, who stood all of about 5'5". We two were most likely no match for the three, both in the art of pool and that of bar room cleanout via a standard brawl ... and a brawl would undoubtedly bring us face to face with the MPs and unit commander.

I thought: what to do? Landi took over. His close friend, Jud, a fellow Warrant Officer, many years senior to the lot of us, sat at the bar, looking into his beer, brooding, as was his usual mode. Rumor held he had served throughout WWII, and even before, as a member of "Merrill's Marauders." Landi was a Warrant Officer, grade W1; and Jud, a W4, the top grade.

Landi asked the three lads to wait a minute, as he would invite his friend to come, make a threesome to engage in the game. The scene was interesting. Landi strode to the bar, reached up, high, put his hand on a huge shoulder, addressed Jud, who turned with a lightly startled look, saw Landi, and said, "Hi, little buddy. What's up?"

"Mister Judson, Sir," in common military parlance to address a senior warrant officer as Landi now did, "we have three gentlemen wishing to engage the lieutenant and me in a pay-for-score game of pool. Perhaps, you would care to make it a threesome?" Jud said he would just rather sit and drink his beer. Landi continued, "Mister Judson, Sir, the gentlemen insist on a game."

What it was, I do not exactly know. Perhaps the actual vocabulary, choice of words; perhaps their intonation; perhaps Landi's body language, communicated the situation and a plea: Help me out of this pickle! At any rate, Jud then said, "Well, I guess I can join in" as he rose from his stool, and, after pulling himself to his full height and military demeanor, stood a head at least above anyone else in the bar, a formidable 7' plus, an over 300-pound stack of muscle, no flab, just a huge man seemingly up to most any task. He strode with Landi back to the table, and inquired as to who wanted to play.

The locals, sensing a shift in the power projection equation, said they did, and split up. Jud informed them that we would decline their offer, and counter-offered, "Beat it." One of the three had moved behind Jud and hit him on the back of the head with a pool cue. The effect was not as expected. Jud turned to him slowly, said that was hardly a gentlemanly gesture, stepped toward the lad, and lifted him from the floor, one enormous hand on the lad's groin and the other on his throat, eliciting therefrom a most agonizing, high-pitch, high-volume screaming.

The other two jumped Jud from the rear. It had no effect. Jud simply strode, all three aboard, to the pool table, slammed the first down hard on it, turned away, bent down forward and with one hand took a second lad by the rear of the neck, pulled him over his back and threw him to the floor, admonished him to wait his turn.

He made a similar move with the third, pulled him to a standing position, grasped and lifted him in a fashion similar to the first, but from the rear, and marched him ceremoniously toward the door, which Landi had opened. Jud simply threw the chap out, down the approximately twenty - step external stairway, and turned, just in time. The number two lad was preparing to attack. A mighty back - handed slap sent the poor idiot violently against the wall, slumping toward the floor, stunned. Landi simply dragged him to the door and tumbled him down the stairs.

The first lad was now recovering, saw Jud slowly coming toward him, decided wisely the odds were not good, so attempted to pass Jud and exit. Jud agreed with his plan, and assisted with a mighty kick, sending him, too, down the stairway.

There rose from the bottom of the stair a good deal of cursing. Jud positioned himself facing the front of the bar, alongside the doorway, not visible from outside, and simply wiped his lips. A clattering and more cursing followed, with one of the chaps running back up the stairs. He entered the doorway, met a mighty hand and arm swinging 'round, catching him in the face, and sending him backwards down the stairs to the parking lot below. Jud continued his stance as before. More cussing could be heard, then the sound of a few Harleys starting up and growling off into the night. Quiet settled in for several minutes. Landi closed the door.

Jud returned to his stool, looked into his mug, and said, "Ma damned beer's flat!" Landi, having walked with Jud to the bar, said, "Lieutenant!" and repeated Jud's statement. I addressed the help. "Barkeep! A beer!" and pointed to Jud's mug.

It had been an interesting night, and a great honor to have bought Jud a beer.

Eleven

Times were nice then. We had been married over a decade, no children yet, though two would come some few years hence. We worked in the city, at the same government facility, she on the fourth floor, and I on the seventh. Morning and evening we commuted by bus, later by subway when it opened, two strap hangers, a pair of sardines stuffed into a large metal container rolling along the commuter route.

Each noontime we met, had lunch at one of many small local cafeterias – just two humans, man and woman, in love, enjoying each other's company. We rode a bus route, the number eleven, of a private line known as "AB&W," initials for three of the small bedroom communities it served, known more affectionately as "Almost Beats Walking."

Mornings we boarded at its very last pickup point, managed somehow to get into it, our route at that time once making the local news for having carried ninety-six fares aboard a forty-nine seat bus. I recall … the driver would pull up, stop, open the door and shout, "Free beer in the rear," jocularly suggesting that if everyone would just shove a bit rearward, we could pack in the last few commuters. And daily, we were thus sucked aboard, held in when the door closed behind us, and bounced along the non-stop express route, twelve more miles into the city.

More than once we joked about the situation, mentioned that if someone fainted, it would not be noticed until the first stop in the city, where as the pack decompressed with some exiting, there would be a 'plop' to the floor as the 'faintee' finally found enough room to fall. But, if memory serves, I recall no such incident.

On one occasion, making small talk, I jokingly whispered into her ear, "I should eat a hearty meal of cabbage and beans the night before, and smoke a few three-for-a-nickel cigars before boarding the bus."

"Why?" she asked.

"So I can get my own seat."

She said I would probably get my own *bus*, but then would need to drive and find a place to park, thus destroying the advantage of mass-transit commuting. My well-laid plan was dashed before it could be put into action. What a pity.

There came a cold, rainy, and dark winter early evening. We boarded, homeward bound. Thankfully our pickup point was the route's starting point, a city park about three blocks from work. We sat, became packed in with fellow commuters as it filled up, loaded at its last city stop, and lumbered toward the express route out of town.

Now the AB&W Company had a dictum that every driver should know every route. So as we passed a major intersection just before the expressway, directed by a traffic cop, the driver made a right turn – a faux pas. As he did so, a loud chorus of simultaneous, "Hey!" rang out. The driver quickly recognized his error, swung the wheel to a hard left, made a U-turn behind the intersection's traffic cop, then a hard right and back to the proper direction and road, all in one graceful ballerina-type move. The cop just stood there; jumped aside a bit, waved the bus on, and scratched his head for a second or two before returning to his duties.

It seems that driver was not quite used to the eleven routes. We lumbered out the expressway in the lane reserved for busses, and danged if we didn't pass by our exit. Another chorus of, "Hey!" but

Michael Toia

there was no easy and quick correction to this one. On we rolled, and exited a mile further along onto a major highway. The driver planned on making a U-turn, or at least a series of lefts, but each intersection was marked prominently as "No U-Turn" and "No Left Turn." So, he eased over to the right, turned right into a side street – a cul-de-sac!

Well! This was a bit of a pickle. No one had yet disembarked, the bus was packed, and the windows steamed because of the weather. The driver had little option. He turned into the driveway of one house to stop, back up, and get turned about. Two commuters got off, directed his action, and re-boarded.

The house's front room curtain parted, and a man's startled face peered out into the scene. A wag on the bus intoned, "Listen to him! I bet he's saying, 'For gosh sakes, Martha … freshen your makeup; we have company.' " All aboard agreed that this was just another of AB&W's occasional unscheduled tours, and had a bit of a giggle over it. I do yet, to this day.

Golf

This is a story of love, true love, and how I met my daughters' mother.

Having just then graduated with a bachelor's degree in science and a commission as a reserve officer in the Army, I had neither wife nor girlfriend of any sort. The last year of college, with a forty-hour work week needed to pay the bills, took my full time and attention. The schedule was bereft of spare time. But now the degree was *fait accompli*, spare time reappeared on the schedule, so a call to a former girlfriend seemed in order. Alas! In the intervening year she had married!

I knew not what to say, how to say it, or how to say anything. I stammered a "congratulations," which expressed my surprise. She laughed, said it was a very small intimate wedding with only immediate family, so how was I to know? But, she continued, she had a close girlfriend, had never introduced the two of us, said to give her a call, and passed me her phone number. I tried to beg off, said I didn't know the girl, and wouldn't be so bold as to do such a thing. She insisted and said, "You call her, buster, and you will marry her!" I scoffed. No way. Then she *dared* me.

The die was cast.

The call was placed. An oh-so-sweet feminine voice answered, caught my attention, chatted a bit, and then agreed to a date the following Saturday evening. At the appointed time I located her home, some ten or so miles from mine at the time, and then rang the bell. A beautiful face on a graceful, girlish frame answered. I was taken quite aback. Something in my psyche just went "POW!" as the unexpected vision rushed my senses. As I think back on the moment, it was a case of love at first sight.

The evening was wonderful. Per our telephonic prearranged plan, we had a skate date. She seemed to enjoy it. I enjoyed her company considerably, so much so as to ask her if she would like to go out again the next weekend. To my pleasureful surprise, she agreed.

The next weekend came. Our date came and went. It was even more enjoyable than the first, and the dates on the next few weekends were all the more so. As it happened, I finally heard of employment, some 400 miles to the east, so we had a final get-together before my departure. I knew her street address and phone number; she gave me her mailing address – P.O. Box 244. A courtship of telephone calls and letters developed. The letters, in particular, did it. That young lady could really write; kept me keenly interested. This led to weekend road trips back to the home area, and further dating.

It was not long, just a few months, when I proposed marriage. She turned me down! It was a rather low point in my life, to be refused by one who had captivated me so. Quite dejected, I returned her to her home, took my leave, and drove the 400 miles to my new residence. I did not return for some time.

I kept in touch with my parents. Mother said the young lady had called a few times, asking if I had come home. I mentioned my proposal and its rejection, said there was little reason for me to keep in touch with the one who had crushed my dreams. Mother told me to call. She had promised she would have me do so.

I called. We spoke a bit. Would I be coming back soon? I said it was not likely, but she asked if I would come so we could talk face to face. I agreed; it was time for a visit to my parents anyway, so there would be no inconvenience, only a heavy heart.

Michael Toia

We had a get-together, just to do nothing – a bit of a drive about the hills, a chat, and a discussion. Of course, her refusal was uppermost on my mind, and apparently hers, too. At the time she was a sophomore in college, seeking a degree in chemistry, and wanted to continue, to earn her degree. That was the reason for her refusal. She asked if we might continue our relationship till then.

We had a long discussion, exploring alternatives. I said I would shortly be called to active duty in the Army for three years, knew not where I would be stationed, how many miles would separate us, and knew that I would likely not have the luxury of weekend visits with her. This could be quite a problem.

Then, still in love with that beautiful, graceful young woman, I explored another alternative. If she would consent to be my wife, we would send her back to college just as soon as we could afford to do so, and in the intervening time we would be together, facing the world as a young duo, experiencing many new things and a deep love.

She accepted this proposal! On her twentieth birthday we two visited an emporium. She picked out her engagement /wedding ring set. I was elated, and on that evening we joined a group of mutual friends at a little party.

Early evening found us at a mini-golf park. I was then, and remain, not a golf aficionado, knew and know little of the game beyond minigolf. She was similarly skilled and interested in the game. However, playing the lead part as the big, strong man in our relationship, and she playing me as someone to protect her, hold her, show her, I wound up behind her, my arms around her, showing her the very little I knew about how to hold a putter and address the ball. I stepped back just a tad. She took a stroke at the ball; with a beautiful follow-through, a complete swing, a beautiful arc, and WHAM! Caught me alongside the head with that iron putter.

I always was starry-eyed around her. This took it to a whole new level. I saw stars, the type not often seen – pain stars. Lots of them. It about knocked me out, as it threw me to the ground.

She turned toward me, saw me holding my head, rubbing the struck area, and looking at my hand for evidence of blood. She was both deeply apologetic and, at the same time, comically amused. A few other friends saw the comic relief of the incident. One came to my aid to examine the damage that, fortunately, was light. As I recovered, I looked at my love, fleetingly wondered if I had made a mistake; *perhaps, she doesn't like me*, is trying to drive me off after having mistakenly agreed to my proposal? I wondered. But, her concern for my well-being outweighed her initial comic response. She, too, came to my aid, apologizing profusely, and we remained a betrothed couple. Later that year we were man and wife.

She knocked me *down* that night. It took twenty years, but I finally evened the score and then some; twice, yet ... two years apart. And that's how I came to have two daughters whose amazing beauty rivals that of their mother; all three the undisputed loves of my life.

Michael Toia

Red Bank

Early in their married life, she presented him with quite a birthday present. She bought him a canoe, a seventeen-foot Grumman standard. They had been canoeing a bit, renting boats as needed, and now had their own. It was awesome, with paddles, life preservers, and car-top carriers to take it wherever they desired.

The local river was a well-used boating recreational area. They put in along its banks at various times, the two of them with their faithful dog, paddled about near a few small islands. She paddled bow ... he, stern. In warm weather, bow paddle would sport one or another of her fabulous bikini collection, a graceful, slender and tall nymph of a woman. He remembers it well.

They would, at times, paddle past a row of small cabin cruisers moored alongside a boat club. She in her usual attire and with dog always attracted attention. Brief greetings with occupants of the other boats were not unusual. Once, the weather scowling deeply and preparing to rain, they made for shore and shelter. As they passed a cruiser, a voice asked, "What do you do when it rains?"

They said, "Go below (decks)."

The dog always sat amid-ship, soaking up water that entered the boat as if a large sponge or the wick of an oil lamp, and it evaporated from his body hair. Once someone asked, "What's the dog's name?" They answered, "Bilgewick." It was essentially true and, in fact, his nickname; after all, the dog did soak up bilge water.

Came a mid-December day, they put in at a new spot, a few miles downriver. Though the weather was on the cold side, the outing was nonetheless enjoyed. They both wore warm jackets. This was hardly bikini weather. Dog, of course, was already well insulated, with his double coat, long light tan hair on the outside, and beneath, a felt-like coat of fine creamy white fur a half-inch thick about his whole body. There were no other pleasure boats out; the lot of them having been placed in dry-dock until spring, beyond ice season.

They paddled past a local boat club. The wharves had already been pulled in for the winter. The river was now clear of most such structures. A voice from the river bank hailed, "Ahoy, the canoe!" and its owner waved them to come closer. They did. The hailer engaged them in conversation, said this was a club dedicated to canoeing, and anyone with enough love of the sport to be on the river this time of year would be really welcome members.

They beached the boat. Their newfound friend showed them about the grounds, through the club house. It was a very old structure, having stood there some five decades. It caught their fancy. The hailer sponsored them and that early spring they were members.

It really was a true canoe club. Canoe and sail boats, no power boats permitted, no bar, no alcohol, a true canoe lovers' association, and they grew rapidly to love it, and to participate in its many activities, especially the many daytrips that were frequent events.

Myriad small streams and creeks flowed westward from the mountains to the east, toward the mighty river. In summer they were small, shallow. One could easily step into or across them. In the early spring, though, the snowmelt made them quite different in character. Each spring the club sponsored a daytrip about every Saturday, an hour or three's drive to a put-in along one of these streams, a five to ten mile cruise downstream to a take-out point, carpooling from one to another, and the cruise itself. These began with a 6 A.M. gathering on the club grounds, an 8 A.M. arrival at the put-in, an hour's car shuttle to the takeout, and return of one car with all drivers to the put-in, then the launch. Après cruise another driver brought the shuttle driver to put-in to retrieve his car.

Mid-April, Red Bank Creek: A rather long cruise began with a 9 A.M. launch, a flotilla of a dozen or so canoes in single file negotiating the mild whitewater to a lunch stop at about 1 P.M. on a wide bank. It was a wet, cold, mid-spring day, rainy. However, little would deter this group from a canoe cruise, and nothing did. They arrived at the lunch stop.

Everyone was chilled and wet. Their ponchos had done what they could, but misery soaked through nonetheless. Canoeists broke out their lunch kits – sandwiches, crackers, cheese, and some sausage. And she, bow-paddle, having planned for such a day, had him, stern-paddle, break out their two waterproof field kitchen containers, and set up a pair of single-burner Coleman gasoline stoves. These little burner units came with, and nested in, an aluminum pot with an aluminum lid that served as a skillet.

The two were gassed up from small metal fuel containers in the kit. She filled both pots with water from their water bags, brought them to a boil, and in one she added some instant noodle soup. The other provided hot water for instant coffee or tea, both of which that clever bow-paddle had packed along in copious quantity.

Shortly the aroma of the soup and coffee wafted about. A close friend noticed, and remarked that that looked more appetizing than his cold lunch. So she asked if he would like some of either. He politely declined, saying he could not take our lunch. Nevertheless, she insisted, pulled out about fifty paper cups from her kitchen kit, a container of instant noodle soup that could feed a hundred, and equal amounts of coffee, tea, powdered creamer, and sugar.

Yes, that day bow-paddle babe ran a soup kitchen, fed just about everyone in the flotilla their heart's content of hot soup, coffee, and tea, along with a goodly supply of saltine crackers, jam, and peanut butter. She was an amazing and resourceful woman, a real "keeper." And I, stern-paddle, did so. That event occurred over forty years ago.

Still, she tolerates me as her mate. We yet own that Grumman canoe. She is still my bow-paddle, and still sports one from her most alluring bikini set on hot summer days. She is yet, and remains the most fascinating, shapely woman to occupy such a position. I remember it well. I experience it in the warm summers to this day.

Michael Toia

No Sale

Once in our life we, childless husband and wife of two decades, decided to chuck our careers, and so did. We purchased and moved to a small farm in a Florida backwater county, and established a small business. Alas! We found after the move that we had made our new home in "the baby house," as the locals called it. Everyone who ever lived in that little place had babies. And lo! It happened to us, as well. We were overjoyed, graced with two tiny daughters, the absolute delight of our lives. Meanwhile my wife, going through eighteen months of pregnancy and subsequent motherhood of the two little darlings, did what she could to assist in the business, but, of course, her time was needed elsewhere.

We acquired a franchise, opened a small store, selling wares of the home company, and she cleverly opted that we would also establish a video rental operation. The store sold electronic knick-knacks, higher end items not terribly profitable, but small items, particularly batteries, carried a good deal of the water. We added a video rental operation, the brainchild of my spouse, and it was quite a hit. We built a rental fleet of six machines and several hundred movie titles, the latter being my wife's choice. Her rentals returned much to the business.

I also farmed out my talents elsewhere, catered to a number of local small AM and FM broadcast stations as a part-time maintenance engineer on call. These stations were 'mom-n-pop' operations that could scarcely afford the talents of a full-time engineer. This augmented our income, and between it, the store, and some investment interest from our previously earned and saved income of the past two decades, we kept going, not extravagantly, but with our head above water for the time spent there.

The store sales were small. We were licensed to collect sales tax for the state of Florida, and were required to make monthly payments of taxes so collected. This we did. Payments were due on the twentieth of the following month, and there were penalties for late payment. We dutifully complied and mailed our tax statement with the required check by the sixth of each month, allowing fourteen days for the mail to deliver our payment.

The first month's cycle occurred. In a rather short time, a missive was received from the state, indicating that our taxes were not received by the twentieth, and demanding a late filing fee of fifty dollars. Fifty dollars! Our sales for the month were on the order of two thousand dollars, with tax due on the order of one hundred twenty dollars. A fifty dollar excess tab took food from the mouths of our babies! We complained, by telephone and letter, to no avail; the state had far more legal horsepower than we could possibly muster. We paid the penalty.

Subsequent filings were forwarded certified mail, return receipt requested. The receipts did return showing payment received at Tallahassee well before the twentieth of each month. Nonetheless, the dunning notice demanding late filing fee was also received, religiously, each month. Armed with proof of timely payment, we sent a follow-up letter to Tallahassee indicating that we had a US Post Office receipt showing that we had paid on time. Each month a representative from Tallahassee would stop by the store, we would produce the receipt, and he would negate the demand for penalty. This continued the entire time we operated the store.

Now, when living on a small income and self employed, medical insurance was terribly expensive and paid meager benefits. We were reimbursed ninety dollars per baby delivery to pay for hospital expenses, and the same for the doctor's fee, though the actual costs were $1,200 and $750, respectively. Then babies become ill, run a fever, get a rash, whatnot. My wife and I could judge our degree of self-illness, and whether we could just treat it and work it out without a doctor or hospital visit; but babies … they can't do the same and communicate it to the parents, so we found need of a better health care plan. I put my talents to work, drafted a resume, and searched for employment. Shortly thereafter I was on the payroll of the Air Force at Robins AFB, GA. Our little ones decided to move to Macon, GA, and we followed them.

Our store and video rental business continued to operate, under the care of a good manager whom we trusted. But eventually he, too, found it necessary to move on, as his wife had a baby; they experienced the same conditions that beset us. We reached a decision. Our small business was not profitable enough, so we closed down. What inventory that could be sold off, even at a loss, was sold. We prepared a final state sales tax statement and forwarded it to Tallahassee with the usual return receipt request, and as usual the receipt indicated our payment had arrived well before the twentieth of the following month.

In short order we received the standard, monthly dunning notice, with demand for late payment. It seems Tallahassee had a racket going in this regard. One would think someone there should experience prison life for several years over the issue. As far as is known, this never happened. We answered the notice as usual, giving our Macon, GA address.

Tallahassee's response was that they could not come to Macon, and assessed additional penalties. This continued for several months, their demand now rising to over four hundred dollars. We were getting nowhere with the matter. We found ourselves between the proverbial rock and a hard spot. Then an inspiration hit us. I visited the local post office, was allowed a short visit with the postmaster to explain that we were victims of apparent mail fraud. He directed me to the US Marshall's office on the second floor, where I explained the situation, and presented the stream of dunning notices, the receipts, sales tax records, and canceled checks for payment thereof.

Things became interesting. He agreed. He asked if it would be a terrible financial hardship on our family to pay the tax. I at first protested, said we did not owe the tax. He continued. Write a check. Pay the tax. Include a letter stating that the tax is paid under protest, and receipt of the canceled check will initiate a filing of mail fraud in the county of Bibb, GA, whose seat was Macon. This action would clear our case in Tallahassee, as the demanded penalties were paid. It would then move the matter to Bibb County, GA, and Tallahassee would need to come here to argue a case of mail fraud that they would lose. Interesting. So we prepared a check and letter, and consigned both to the US Mail, return receipt requested.

Two weeks later, we received another mailing from Tallahassee. It contained our original check – not processed! It contained a notice that they had seen the error of their ways, and that all was forgiven.

Ah, yes. If one can work out the route, one can use the government to hold itself at bay in defense of the common man. And this process is that which fuels the lawyer business, the business of those who make laws so twisted that one need hire their fellow lawyers for self defense. Reminds one of the story of two boys walking down a dirt road one early fall. They spied a walnut in the middle of the road, reached it simultaneously, and argued in vain over its possession. They sought the advice of a mutual friend, a boy both accepted as a good deal more intelligent than the sum of their intellects.

The third considered a bit, and then divided the walnut neatly in two halves. He gave each boy one half of the shell, and kept the nutmeat as his fee. He likely now has a very successful legal practice, continuing this stratagem at our expense. So it goes with lawyers.

Michael Toia

Solar

Too many years past, I was a younger man, married, and in the early part of my career. As a technocrat, all things geeky in nature caught my attention. Then came one of those then-avant-garde devices, a calculator, small enough to be held in the hand, a four-function marvel with red lit numerals. It could add, subtract, multiply, and divide. Such a gem was on the market for the sum of about a hundred and fifty dollars.

That faded quickly. Quite soon the scientific calculator made its debut; it could do trigonometry functions like sine, cosine, tangent, log functions, and on, and on. Its price started at about four hundred, but in a few short years, was offered for as little as nine ninety-five. Yes ... less than ten bucks! How technology changes in such a short time. And now in 2014 we have hand-held computers of sheer ability and power many orders of magnitude above that that guided the Lunar Landing Module on July 20, 1969.

When the price dropped below twenty dollars, practically everyone – student, office worker, housewife – acquired one or more. Schools began to require students to buy a particular brand or model of calculator to engage in the curriculum of a given class.

Nowadays, the landfills have already been stuffed with many of those early marvels, and I dare say there are several lurking about in forgotten drawers, boxes, nooks, and crannies in just about every home in the nation. In untold numbers, survivors still find daily use in balancing household finances, and my beautiful spouse gives example of such use. She has small calculators sitting next to our few home computers, and a couple in the kitchen, where she runs various numbers while internet shopping, checkbook managing, home financial planning, and sundry other daily uses.

Early models of these cute widgets ran on nine volt batteries. Technology advanced. The calculator lost weight, became thinner, thinner, and much thinner than that battery. The later ones were powered by a coin cell, about the size of a quarter or dime, supporting that thinner, flatter physical format, and along the way came a calculator that had no batteries. It was powered by small solar cells just above its display, and my spouse acquired her first solar, just such a calculator, then a few others.

The moniker "solar" applied to those powered by tiny solar cells that ran on available light. But not all people are geek-technocrats, and quite get the point. I often came home, walked into our dining room to gaze out at a beautiful view – a two-acre yard of amazing trees, seclusion, filtered sunlight dancing in the shade, with the sun off to the west, now streaming through a patch of bamboo wafting to and fro in a light breeze, thru the dancing shadows and into the room … and what did my eyes perceive? Calculators. Solars. Lined up on the windowsill. Why, I asked?

My sweets explained. They are solar calculators, so need sunlight. The dining room table is her preferred desk during the day, where she sorts the mail, pays bills, writes checks, peruses catalogs, and performs related activities. And, as its large window faces West, the calculators are so placed to benefit from their much needed late day sunshine … and of this she is convinced. Her argument is so reasonable, I'm happy they are not aquasolar calculators, or they would be watered, too.

As an engineer, I did my best to explain that, although the word solar is, indeed, part and parcel of their design, it doesn't take sunlight to operate them. Rather, initial research was aimed at capturing solar energy and converting it to useful electricity. Then the

Michael Toia

application of tiny solar cells to other devices followed. In fact, those calculators can run on ordinary room light or in the windowless basement of an office building without ever seeing the sun. But some people are not techno-geeks, and simply do not "dig it." And my wife, beautiful and gorgeous as she is, is in the latter category, with by far the majority of the populace. To this day our windowsill is the repository of her solar calculators. Moreover, I had introduced another element of curious concern to her.

That particular type of calculator has no 'On/Off' button that she can discover. Therefore, it will wear out soon, deplete its battery, and die. Explanation to the contrary invokes recall of Douglas Adams' famous statement in *Hitchhiker's Guide*: "Resistance is useless." But to her credit, she trusted me, and made a good-faith attempt to understand that, when the light fails, such as when the device is set in a dark desk drawer, or at night, the calculator stops. It shuts down. OFF. Automatically.

The next evening she countered my argument. She had taken one of her "solars" with her to the back of a large closet, the closet light off. Then she discovered the characteristic of liquid crystal displays. They don't give off light. The display was totally dark. Invisible. She could not tell if the calculator had, in fact, shut itself off. So, she repeated the procedure, her experiment, took a flashlight into the closet, and used it to illuminate the calculator.

Lo! It was not OFF. It was still working! So my explanation had to be wrong. The calculator would wear itself out. So there must be an On/Off switch on it somewhere, but she had yet to discover it. Of course, the feeble illumination of the flashlight was enough to power the device! At least that's my explanation. But … maybe she's right, and I'm wrong?

I solved the problem. I bought her a calculator that runs on those small coin cell batteries. It needs not sunshine. Nor watering. And has an 'On/Off' button.

Matchmaker

Though I never had thought of myself as a matchmaker, nor Cupid, I've had the great honor of "arranging" three matches, including Joyce and myself, that each lasted more than fifty years.

Case #1: Jeannie - The Girl Next Door

Approaching my fourteenth birthday, my family moved to a new town. There was a new school to attend, and therein a young lady named Donna Jean. She played the viola, I, the string bass. She played the alto horn, I, the baritone. Her home was one block distant, on the daily walk to and from school. We became friends, and a few years later began dating. Would she, perhaps, be the one? To this day she is called Jeannie, my nickname for her back in that day. But a continuing romance was not to be.

College introduced a new friend, Joe, and that friendship developed deeply. We frequently double-dated ... he with another, and I, with Jeannie. One evening, on bidding good-night on her front porch, I found Jeannie tongue-tied and awkward, even though we'd known each other five years at that time. She fumbled for words, wanting to ask me a favor, but feeling awful about it. I assured her our friendship would last, no matter what. So, she blurted it out, haltingly: Could I bring Joe around more often? Flabbergasted, I asked, "Are you sweet on Joe?" She confessed, "Y-y-yes." So, I complied. We still double-dated; Joe with Jeannie, and I with a different friend of hers on just about every date. She was trying to repay a favor, but none caught.

In 1958 Jeannie turned eighteen ... and disappeared for a time. She and Joe had eloped! They are still man and wife, with two children, and grandchildren. And, they still live just a few blocks from her former home. And yes, indeed, we are still friends. Joyce and I just visited her a few weeks back, the end of summer, August 2014.

Case #2: Judy - A Mentor's Daughter

Lee had just moved to town, and we met one late afternoon by ham radio. My home at the time was on the North side of a hill overlooking a small stream. Lee lived in the adjoining town, the stream being the boundary line. We spoke. He described his house. I could see it from my window, a half mile away, on the South slope of the same stream valley.

As he was new in town, I invited him to come, attend the local ham club meeting. He begged off at first, but after some prodding, accepted. Despite the three decades separating us, we became close friends. And as that friendship proceeded, Lee spoke of his son Sid, then serving in the Navy. He mused that the two of us, Sid and myself, seemed to have a lot in common and, perhaps, one day might meet.

A year later, Sid completed his Navy hitch and returned home. We met. Lee was right. There was instant friendship, mutual acceptance, and as time went on, we became very close, did almost everything together. I introduced Sid to the local radio hams, one of whom, Bill, was a WWII vet, a retired Army Air Force radio operator who spent a good part of the war as an NCO at a major radio relay station at Goose Bay, Labrador.

Our routine found us at Bill's place frequently. The mutual

interest in ham radio was a strong attraction. Bill had many wartime stories to relate, appreciated by an eager and accepting audience, and we were such. He had five daughters, Sharon the youngest still at home in high school, and Judy the next youngest away in the Air Force. As time passed, Judy returned home, became a regular on our double-dating, accompanying Sid.

One early evening I called Sid. We had planned on visiting Bill. I was surprised to hear he had already departed about an hour ago. It was a scant ten-minute drive from his home to mine ... had he been in an accident? I drove the route to his home, but no accident, no Sid. I drove the six miles to Bill's place, only to meet and chat with Bill. No Sid. He and Judy had earlier departed together.

Aha! The plot thickened. Judy had cast her spell on my friend, and in just a few months I was asked: would I be his best man? Of course I would, and one November 5, I had the great honor of being a member of the wedding party; Judy and Sid, the marriage of my best friend. And, he reciprocated in kind the very next month, New Year's Eve.

Alas, not long after, we parted ways – he off to Seattle in search of employment and I off to New Jersey, also in search. Over the years we kept in touch, sometimes sporadically, but never lost contact with each other. Many years later, as he and Judy honored us with a visit to our home, I had the pleasure of announcing to our dinner table company – the two of them, their daughter Sheryl, my two daughters, and my heartthrob – that I was most fortunate. I had made friends, some of whom were close friends, and two best friends, the woman in the kitchen, and the gentleman sitting next to me.

Sid and Judy lived in the Seattle area, and celebrated their golden anniversary; a month later in Las Vegas, with my sweetie and I, a double golden wedding anniversary.

The third and final story of this sequence follows:

Case #3: Joyce - My True One-and-Only

I've already told this story under the title *Golf.* For periodic updates on that romance, read *AXX12, Honey, Red Bank, Mephisto,*

Eleven, Red, Casino, and *V2* in my series of tales. Wow! Truly a woman of *je ne sais quoi* who totally captured my heart, and holds it tight to this very day, fifty-three years after our wedding, and counting.

I paraphrase Mark Twain's so eloquent statement, placing it in the present tense: "Wheresoever she is, there is Eden."

Tierra del Fuego

Our firstborn graced us with a son-in-law, and not too soon after, the two graced us further with a sweet, wonderful grand-daughter. When she, the little one, was not yet five months into the world, their little family unit moved to Florida, temporarily. Our new son's employer sent him forth to fit a satellite to a launch vehicle, and Cape Canaveral was chosen to be the launch site.

We, residents of Northern Virginia, missed our daughter, our new son, and the little one. So, a vacation plan was set in motion, and to Florida we went, to the mid-Atlantic coast at Cocoa Beach, to spend a week with the trio. We flew to Melbourne via Atlanta.

Now, wife and I once lived in Florida, in the Panhandle on the way to Pensacola, half past Tallahassee, where one must cross the Apalachicola along the way from Tallahassee's airport, and in so doing, enter the central time zone. And, at that time and place, in a faraway backwater county of the state, came our two little ones into the world, two daughters, two years apart, the first of whom was the subject of our planned trip.

Earlier in life, as newlyweds, we were guests of the US Army, and spent two years living in Georgia. Some twenty-five years later, we found ourselves again in Georgia, as residents of Macon, center of the state, a beautiful, small, very ante-bellum old-South city with a charm rivaling that of Savannah. We loved the place, and considered returning thereto in retirement.

Back in time, about a half century ago, Disney World and Orlando were not as much a destination as now, and though the airline industry was well established, it was yet to grow much larger. Atlanta, its old Hartsfield Airport, was then, as now, a major hub, and whatever air travel was planned to the Southeast invariably involved a transfer at Atlanta, so much so that the local quip was, "When your time on Earth is up, it matters not which way you go, you'll go to Atlanta for connections." So it was, and is today, with Melbourne.

The appointed day arrived. Wife had packed what we needed for a week. She has always been not only my love and heartthrob, but my attendant, as well, in all details, including packing my bags for every business trip I have ever taken or will take. I cannot recall any incident where some item needed on a trip was not in my luggage at the time and place of need. She is that thorough.

At 10 A.M we departed the house, drove to the airport, found a spot and parked the car, waited for and caught the shuttle, and made it to the terminal. Then it was off to the ticket kiosk, baggage check, and TSA. Ahh, yes … TSA. Empty the pockets. Off with the belt and shoes. Put everything into a Tupperware tub. Step into the scanner machine. Place both hands over the head. Wait until the machine does its thing. Then reach down, pick up pants from about the ankles, hold them up, leave the machine, retrieve the Tupperware tub and stuff with one hand, and try to put everything back in your pockets, the other still holding the trousers. Then walk off twenty feet, sit down, put on shoes and belt. At this point, a senior female TSA officer admonished me about having indecently exposed my undies and, perhaps, more. Ahh, yes, the sheer dignity of it all.

Then off on a long, long hike, down escalators, onto shuttle trains, off the trains, up escalators, and off to gate one gazillion, somewhere beyond the end of the gate areas, it would seem. Now in my youth that was a good workout, but I'm off to see my granddaughter. So, a youth I wasn't at this time. Rather, I've survived a heart attack, a quad bypass, and carry a handicap placard for my auto. Nevertheless, after a brief sit-down spell to renormalize my heart and panting rates at gates one million, two million, and three million, there I arrived – gate one gazillion – huffing, puffing, and a bit dizzy.

Oh, yes, I know. I could get one of those little gate-area shuttles, except for three things. First, they are usually not around. Then they have no room. And, finally, when I get to that stage of life, I know I will have less than one year left to go. So, I resist with all my might. I resisted my doctor's advice to apply for a handicap placard for the auto. I protested, "I'm not handicapped."

He said, "On days you aren't, don't use it. On days you feel you might be, use it."

Dang! 'Tis amazing how fast you get used to those things. Hence, my stubbornness to ride through airports, and my spouse's concern for me.

Now, we find a flight delay of unknown length; some sort of mechanical difficulty. A wait of a half hour or more, then a gate change, and finally we are allowed to board an airplane, destination Atlanta. It's 4:30 P.M. We've been in travel mode since ten; six and a half hours, and we're already twelve miles from the house.

By 6:30 we were at Hartsfield. Despite our late departure, the wisely preplanned two hour overlay enabled getting aboard the Melbourne flight comfortably. It ran on time, and later that evening we were at baggage claim, then the car rental counter at our final destination. By 10:15 we now had ground transportation and were on our way to the hotel, close by, and at 10:45 had finally made it to our room, only a bit over twelve hours from leaving the house.

We had a wonderful visit with our spawned family unit, a good chat with daughter and son-in-law, and, of course, a lot of time with our little granddaughter Hannah. Weather was Florida standard – nice, warm, not hot, and with the nearly scheduled afternoon thundershower. Our visit spanned the Fourth of July, so we watched a few fireworks displays from the balcony of the high rise that son-in-law's firm had rented for his stay there.

One evening we decided to see if a restaurant I had visited many times before was still in business, and still a nice place. An internet search confirmed that, indeed, it still did exist. We decided to seek it out.

My age now came to the fore. I do not recall the place being so far, so long a drive, as it now appeared. Somehow the Earth had expanded since my last visit, or the roads got longer, or, perhaps, I just drive more slowly than in ages past. But we did subsequently get there in time to enjoy an unhurried meal. I mentioned that the trip seemed so much farther than I remembered, and quipped that we might have tried a restaurant closer by, such as Milliways. [10] Son-in-law laughed instantly, catching in a flash my lightly disguised sarcasm. Nonetheless, the place had been my choice!

Then, as usual, a delightful visit had hurried by far too fast, and our return trip came about. Pack up. Check out. Say goodbye. And off to Melbourne it was, for a 4 P.M. departure, delayed, for the incoming aircraft, low on fuel and routed away from the local thunderstorm, was directed to nearby Orlando to gas up. By about 5:30 we were finally aboard and took to the air. We were a bit late into Atlanta, but again my spouse's wisely planned two and half hour overlay allowed us to board the homeward bound flight in a comfortable and unhurried manner, even allowing time for my hike, slowly, from gate to gate with necessary rest stops of a minute here, a minute there. Finally, about 10 P.M. we were again in the air, on our last leg.

Now began that long, long expedition back through our home airport, from gate one gazillion and one, to the escalators, down to the train, to the terminal stop, up a bank of escalators, through the security doors and on to baggage claim, and thereafter through the terminal, out to the shuttle bus stop, the ride to the pay lot, to our car, to the checkout lane, and payment of a mere sixty dollar ransom. By 3 A.M. we were finally home, crashing in bed.

I awoke later the following morning, and after a nice brunch prepared by my sweetie, decided to call at the office to catch up on a week of e-mails, crises, notes, demands, etc. It was then that I noticed my throat seemed a bit scratchy. The next two days I spent in sick bay, coughing up gobs of what-not from my lungs ... hacking, wheezing, unable to catch my breath at times. After a weekend of the same, a visit to the doctor's office, a diagnosis of

---

[10] D. Adams, *The Restaurant at the End of the Universe.*

acute bronchitis, a prescription, and five days of an antibiotic regime, with more time missed at work, all transpired.

Honestly, flying seems not to be such a great way to travel, stuffed into a big metal tube for a few hours at a crack, half the fellow travelers breathing in as the other half breathed out, exchanging what germs someone had brought aboard, and resulting in an illness of several days after the ordeal.

I don't like to fly.

I'd rather drive.

How far can it be to Patagonia?

West

Used to be, airlines sponsored mini-vacations – three or four-day getaway packages. You called the airline. They made all the arrangements – rental car, hotel, ticketing. We had taken a few in earlier years and enjoyed each one. Nearing burnout after a year of setting up a new regional office, I was ready. 'Twas May of '72.

Joyce, my darling spouse of several years at the time, called United and booked four days in Denver. Rocks and minerals fascinated us at the time. We had completed two semesters of basic and advanced cabochon cutting at a local trade school, reputed to be one of the finer in the country, in the Western suburbs of Chicago. We were graduate lapidaries. So another rock-hounding vacation it was to be.

While in the area we did the standard tour up Pike's Peak. The monument at the top bespeaks 14,110 feet elevation. A lie! A friend and colleague at the time, who hailed from Colorado, related that his great uncle, a surveyor, had the distinction of having measured a good bit of land near the mountain, and said the elevation was 14,109 – a full foot less. The state tourism industry is apparently wont to exaggeration.

Arriving at the peak, my spouse and I discovered that we were Easterners, hardly ever having lived at elevations above 800 feet. We were air breathers, and there wasn't much to breathe. It was thin. We sat in the car for several minutes, a bit dazed, somewhat in a dream world, yet cognizant of where we were, but unable to move in that automatic sense one uses to walk about, chew gum, etc.

In a short time, as best as I can estimate, I spoke to myself, said I needed to get out of the car, and so directed my actions by mentally speaking to my body as if a drill sergeant, moved my arm, opened my door on verbal command, directed my left foot out onto the ground and continued, by the numbers, to extract myself from the car. I found myself standing erect, then by continued verbal drill, marched about the auto and aided my spouse in exiting same.

There we stood a few minutes, trying to shake off the dreaminess, spied a snack bar, and directed ourselves to walk thereto. After a soda or two and a light bite to eat, our dreaminess faded sufficiently, and we now found our automatic walking controls to again function, about eighty percent restored. We enjoyed the view for a half hour or so. I saw the monument, a plaque set horizontally atop a boulder, set in some mortar, announcing the elevation to be 14,110 feet above sea level. Foul! The one-foot bed or mortar is not a part of the Peak, having been brought there from a lower elevation.

All good things must come to an end, and so it was with our visit to the summit. We began a slow, leisurely decent back down the mountain, stopped a few times to examine the local rock and stone, looking for hand samples, but found nothing worthwhile. We discovered that 11,000 feet was about our limit, as full automatic body movement functions returned at that level and below. On finally reaching the bottom, we drove to, and retired in, our motel room.

We spent our few days on the eastern slope of the Rockies, West of Denver, quite a bit along Clear Creek, and did the tourist thing – panned for gold, found none, but found instead a good number of rounded, stream-tumbled ilmenite pebbles, of a deep steel gray color. I gathered a small bagful and packed them away, to try them at our home shop, where we later found they cut well and took a high polish when finished as gem-quality stones.

But I digress. We put in at a tourist mine, one of hundreds in the area. It being a weekday, Joyce and I were the establishment's sole clients. The mine's owner, a pleasant chap by the name of Mr. West, sold us dirt from a pile near the tourist flume. The dirt, of course, was salted. West mixed the gold dust he found into it, sold it to tourists (us) by the bucketful, and got about three times what he could for the gold alone on the open market. Meanwhile, the tourist learned how to pan, actually found gold, and had a wonderful souvenir to take home. Nuggets he sold in his on-site small shop, individually priced according to their weight and character.

We hit pay dirt! Found our share of gold ... and more. There's something about sitting by the flume, fresh and cold mountain water splashing across the pan and hands, slopping it onto one's trousers and shirt; that washes away the trials and troubles of the daily grind. It's amazingly calming. And, the mental rush of anticipating, and seeing gold ... yes, real gold! ... keeps the mind away from daily problems. I highly recommend it.

West lived up in those foothills, did not have a lot of contact with the city, and was a tad lonely. We struck up a conversation while panning away flume-side in that cold, pure spring water. West's great grandfather had come out that way during the 1850's gold rush. Joyce said her great uncles had done the same, and one had stayed in Colorado. West said his family came from Ohio. Joyce said, "My family's from Ohio too." West said it was a small town, named East Palestine.

Joyce rose slowly to her feet. That's her family! Her maiden name is West. Two dumfounded n-th cousins stood there, looking into each others' faces. Joyce told her side of the story. Turned out she and West knew some of the same relatives! The three of us were amazed at the coincidence. Of a hundred tourist mines in those hills, we picked that one.

West said, "If you wanna keep diggin' in the dirt, be my guest. But I'd sure like to show you how the mine works. Don't often get kin visitin'." We got the first-class tour. Unforgettable. All because I went "West" for a bride.

And was this a coincidence? Of those hundred or so tourist mines, were any others owned by descendents of West's great-grandfather ... about half, I'd wager. Possibly more.

Taps

There's a part of Pennsylvania a few score miles southeast of Pittsburgh, in the Alleghenies, known as the Laurel Highlands, named after the state flower, the Mountain Laurel. And, not to be left aside, Laurel Mountain is one of the prominent high ridges running through the area. Straddling it, snuggling the Mason-Dixon Line, rest Somerset and Fayette counties, beautiful regions containing many small towns and villages, several serene mountain parks, numerous small waterfalls, and a number of ski areas. The Youghiogheny River, or the mighty "Yough" (pronounced YOCK), enters from the South, from Maryland, and cuts a gap in Chestnut Ridge, one feature west of Laurel Mountain, through a state park at a dot on the map named Ohiopyle. Many a person knows the area, a center for wild river raft trips, and many a time did we partake thereof.

Eastern Highlands, Somerset County, is a particularly beautiful area, a year-'round vacation Mecca, with about everything one could desire. Hiking, wild-river rafting, canoeing, fishing, golf, and all sorts of other summer amenities aplenty are offered, along with just plain relaxing. Fall brings riots of color from the minions of maple, hickory, oak, and other trees. A beautiful flaming red occurs on a viney plant, poison ivy; these particular leaves are not recommended for picking and collecting! Winter brings skiing, sleigh rides, horseback jaunts, and offers many, many resorts and restaurants that provide every winter recreational activity one could want, both indoors and out.

The former Kaufmann country home, now a conservatory, lies a short distance north of the state park at Ohiopyle. The elder Kaufmann had established a very well-known and respected retail department store in the city, and was one of the more wealthy residents of the area. Supposedly he directed his son, a student of architecture at Northwestern, to seek advice of his professors on building a mountain lodge for entertainment of guests. One professor insisted on a site visit, decided to design a structure spanning a tiny waterfall on a small brook, and in a few years and over a million dollars later there it stood – Fallingwater, the brainchild of professor Frank Lloyd Wright – truly a beautiful blend of man and nature, and absolutely worth the visit. My particular thrill on touring this structure is to find myself standing in the bedroom favored by a distinguished visitor, one Albert Einstein.

Rather reminiscent of Vermont, late winter visitors see thousands of trees alongside the roads and in the towns, sporting buckets, collecting sap from the many maples. As native-born Pittsburgh souls transplanted to the Washington, DC area, we spent many a day in those highlands, in spring, summer, fall, and winter. In particular, the small village of Myersdale holds a maple festival in late winter, and visits to local sugar camps are a feature to experience, observing and learning about the conversion of maple sap to syrup.

Our Maryland yard once supported about a dozen large maples, which I set out to tap one January. A battery-powered electric drill equipped with a 3/8" bit expedited the tapping. The hole, drilled about 2 inches deep through the bark and into the tree's sapwood, sloped about ten degrees above horizontal as it entered. Best results were had from a second-growth clump of six large, silver maples. One hole was set in each of the six trees and, in short order, sap began flowing forth copiously.

The local hardware store sold 3/8" diameter clear plastic tubing. A piece of this was pressed partway into each hole. Sap began dripping from its free end. To collect it, a hole was poked near the top of an empty gallon milk jug, below the cap and alongside its molded handle. The tube, threaded through the hole, admitted the sap and it began to collect at the bottom. The several jugs were tied to the trees with nylon twine, below the tap holes.

To my delight, I found a quart or two of sap in all six jugs each morning, and sometimes found a jug or three overflowing when I returned from work each evening. On a good day, the six taps produced about eight gallons of sap, enough to produce nearly a pint of syrup. Sap collection continued well into February.

Poured into the largest pot we had on hand, the sap was boiled over a camp stove set in the yard. I've been told trying to do it in the kitchen is a good way to remove all the wallpaper, a good deal of interior paint, and soften drywall. Go and visit a "sugar camp" sometime. The sugar shack with its Miller pans steaming away has no paint at all, and even its wood planks look quite weathered.

My cookout proceeded each evening for several hours. As the sap volume decreased, more was added, up to about five times the pot's maximum capacity. For about 95 percent of the run, it seemed that the pot contained only streaming water. But then it took on a light tan color. Toward the end of the boil, events happened more quickly. The sap thickened and started to foam. Attention was needed at this time to check the sugar content of the remaining product. While this can be done with a sugar hydrometer, another way is to check the temperature of the boiling sap and the temperature of plain water brought to a boil alongside it. This compensates for variations in barometric pressure due to weather changes or elevation of the site. When the temperature difference is about 7° F, the sap has been converted to maple syrup.

It took roughly sixty pints, about seven gallons, boiling for two evenings to make a pint of light syrup. This may be too much work for the average person, but "sugaring" can be a fun parent-child project. Besides, the resulting homemade product is a reward in itself! It's delicious on pancakes, waffles, ice cream, and a spoonful or two gives coffee a delicious twist!

There's a bit of a legend about sugaring in the Laurel Highlands. It seems a large food tanker was transporting several thousand gallons of locally-produced syrup along the Pennsylvania

Turnpike, and was involved in an accident. Syrup spilt across the road, necessitating a closure and a cleanup. I believe that part of the story to be true, and recall having heard of it in the area papers and TV news coverage many years ago.

The legend continues. Authorities summoned fire departments and Lions Clubs out a few tens of miles in all directions, several of whom responded and set up roadside kitchens. They cooked up pancakes by the hundreds, distributed them free to stranded motorists, who took the flapjacks to the pavement, blotted it clean, then ate them! No sense wasting such a delicious product. And this is Pennsylvania's entry into the annals of "road-kill" dining.

Seattle

Years gone by engendered in us a special attachment to Seattle. My very best friend, other than my spouse, relocated there not long after the two of us had met and settled down with our respective sweethearts. And there the two couples were; they on the Northwest coast, while employment took us to the Northeast coast, a continent apart. Neither we nor they had much money in those early days, and mutual visits did not come often, or early, though the telephone kept us in touch.

There came a time when my work took me to the city, and a 12-hour unscheduled delay in flight arrangements brought us together for a wonderful evening. As a few more years went by, job travel found me there more often with yet more opportunity for short, but well appreciated visits. Proud of their city they were, and happy to drive about to show visiting friends this and that, the really unique parts that made Seattle, Seattle, and I found it, indeed, a wonderful place.

From my observations, it appeared as a largely blue-collar working city. Many big businesses developed – Microsoft, Amazon.com, United Parcel Service, Starbucks, and on, and on. These were the product of young, talented entrepreneurs whose abilities are the stuff of awe and admiration. But there is, perchance, a flaw in their thinking – they espoused socially liberal values.

On the surface, this is a wonderful thing. Who would deny unwed mothers government support for their fatherless babies? The effect, though, is to generate an entire class of citizenry, mothers without fathers, having as many babies as possible, for each one meant a quantity of government support. More babies ... more money ... and in comes that nasty law of unintended consequences.

The babies do, indeed, have fathers. The fathers have value. Were they present, mother and babies would receive no government checks. They must disappear. Their value is negative ... less than nothing. So, there grows another class of citizenry, the class of less-than-worthless young males. As for me, this demeaning would instill a resentment, an anger at the system, and since I would need to disappear, I might as well take up a life on the dark side of society. Perhaps, this happens. I let you judge.

But, mothers receive support from the government ... and vote. They vote for the ones offering the most. Of course, living off government support is a direct path to wealth ... copious wealth. Like heck it is. These classes of citizen found themselves living in the projects, another government program to house those less fortunate who have no reasonable wealth. And the projects became beautiful portions of utopian city life, a wonderful place where anyone would strive to dwell. Or, did they?

But alas, their occupants discovered they could rip out the copper wiring and plumbing and sell it as scrap. And, could rip out the fixtures, the bathroom toilet, vanity, the stove, refrigerator, even the kitchen sink. These could be sold as junk, providing some source of income. The project residents would destroy one living unit, claim someone broke in and did this, and the government would move them to another, livable unit. And, on it went ... and goes ... until at last the project becomes irreparably destroyed and is finally razed, a failure of a social experiment. In witness thereof I offer two famous examples, the Cabrini-Green and Robert Taylor Homes projects of Chicago, the latter build circa 1962, demolished circa 2000-2010.

The young liberals rebuilt Seattle, in their own image. Social welfare programs of all sorts existed. A great upwelling of heart about the homeless arose. They certainly needed care. As, of course, do the immigrants, known euphemistically as Americans in Waiting, many there in contradistinction to rule of law, and the city is now a Sanctuary City. What heartless person could deny these people the government aid they so needed?

Ahh, yes again … that law of unintended consequences. Government support becomes a drawing card, a magnet, and what occurs? A growing class of these not-yet citizens. Or, are they?

Driven by these forces, the city changed. Spouse and I had a recent visit thereto, took a guided tour of the environs. Still beautiful, I add. But during a stop at Pike Street Market, wife did her thing, looking for souvenirs to take back to our family, while I sat near water's edge on a park bench, simply enjoying the weather which, that day, was warm, clear, and sunny … 'Twas not the rainy season. I had been at that spot years earlier, partaking of the beauty, the aroma of dockside, hint of sea, fish, and a suggestion of salt air.

However, the aroma had changed. The winds of time had done their thing. I now partook of the odors of urine, marijuana, and feces. As there I sat, a good-sized dog approached, dragging a person behind. The canine performed what it was present do to, and did urinate on a post next to my bench, punctuating the aroma quite pungently. I rose, departed the scene, and was happy to re-enter the tour bus parked nearby, to wait out the remainder of our stop.

We continued the day's tour. The operator thereof believed deeply in the city. He said it and/or the state were early to legalize marijuana, to adopt assisted suicide, to sponsor gay rights' parades in which participants march about naked, and to permit gay marriage; it's a sanctuary city welcoming those walking in from other countries, is very tolerant of the homeless, and so on. I looked at my spouse, and remarked, "Gee, what a swell place! What more could one possibly want?"

We had a nice tour. However, the remainder of the afternoon saw us at the rear of the bus, a case of the giggles having infected her due to my comment and, of course, I egged her on, joining in myself.

My very best friend passed on just a few years back. Aside from his widow, herself a very close friend living in the area, I see little reason to return.

Michael Toia

Payday

Many a person starts out in life, full of dreams, energy, ambition ... and broke. Many have taken the time, paid attention during the free schooling given us, and were advantaged by having parents who put them through college. The successful of us studied and learned math in the fourth grade, a harbinger of a commitment to the value of education, learning skills that would serve us well as adults.

Our young life was according to this mold. We met near the end of our college years, fell in love, married, and departed from beneath our parents' wings into the world, penniless. Education propelled me into a job as an engineer, working in a laboratory on myriad radio systems, garnering further education from a troop of elders who mentored the new crop of us young squirts. Time has now turned the tables and, half a century later, I've become one of those elders: it's payback time. Now to mentor the new hires. But let's return to yesteryear and continue this storyline.

In those days the military draft was still a fact and a young man could face abrupt, involuntary call to service without prior notice. This sword of uncertainty hung over the heads of the young male populace. To bring it to terms, many a college man joined the Reserve Officers Training Corps, the ROTC. This finalized the matter; they would not be drafted, would finish their college years, then be called to duty not as an E1 enlistee, but as an O1 officer. And, thereby, I became a US Army second lieutenant.

A delay of near unto a year between graduation and call to active duty found me engaged as a graduate engineer as previously stated. The two of us, husband and wife, began building our life together – paying the bills, and saving what wee bit of money we could, far short of a king's ransom. In fact, it could ransom no one. Then came the call to service.

We packed the few belongings acquired since our wedding, consigned them to a moving company, tossed a suitcase and the dog into the car, and off we went, leaving New Jersey and Georgia bound. Neither of us had earlier been South of the Mason – Dixon Line, save for my 40 day stint in boot camp midway through college. So this was our first great adventure. The Southern states were different, a change from our previous life. Different was good.

And bad. Poverty was apparent here and there along the byways off the main roads. Southern cities were not unlike those we had grown with, modern and old, new and historic, and presented much interest. Probably our most memorable sighting occurred along a Georgia byway, a chain gang – Sheriff's officers with shotguns tending the crew. We had only heard of such prior to that, and did not quite know what to make of it. As we reflect upon it, we feel it is a good thing. The incarcerated get outdoors – some exercise, fresh air, and sunshine – and civilization profits from their labors. Those who had thus labored should be proud of their accomplishment, and society in general owes them thanks. I for one am appreciative of their efforts.

We arrived at the new assignment. I reported for duty, and upon my first hour incurred the ire of two majors, commanding officers of the 39th and 40th Signal Battalions, and two Captains, commanding officers of the 228th and 519th Signal Companies. But that story is best here left to another writing.

Housing on that military post was far from adequate. We were given the princely allowance of $68 per month to pay rent at an off – post residence. Our actual rent for a suitable single bedroom duplex ran $75 per month: we were already going slowly into a hole, and my salary of $222.30 a month covered our living costs. It had to. We had no other income. A weekly night out on the town

Michael Toia

4 POST FINANCE shall arrange sleeping provisions for said Lieutenant.

5 These orders shall remain in effect until said Lieutenant is given the sum of $402.68 in US bills and coinage.

6 Upon completion of item five (5) above, these orders are RESCINDED.

> SIGNED
> WALTER LEVY
> CAPTAIN, US ARMY

Or about as close as I can recollect. Then the Captain barked,

"Lieutenant!"

"Sir?"

"You're off your duty station!"

And with that I saluted, asked to be dismissed, and it was so. Off to post finance I went, the obligatory twenty-six copies of special orders in hand.

At 1608 the Lieutenant behind the desk asked, "You again?"

I presented a copy of my orders. He read. He scratched his head. He said, "We close at 1630! You can't stay here!"

I informed him that, as I was a good deal bigger and heavier than he, he had no option. So, off to his Captain he went. The latter appeared at about 1615. I handed him a copy of my orders, asked about provisions for my bedding down and evening meal. He, too, tried to tell me to leave. I simply said to call the MPs. I'm staying! Curious, though, what would the MPs have done? Orders are orders.

The Captain and Lieutenant's combined genius found a workaround. I was ushered to the Captain's office. The sum of $402.68 was produced in cash, counted out by the Captain, his Lieutenant, and myself. I signed a receipt for the same, and there-upon was requested to leave. The orders now being rescinded and taking the cash in hand, I did so. It was 1630. The Captain and Lieutenant locked the door behind me.

I returned to the company area. Captain Levy spotted me arriving. He barked at me,

"Lieutenant! You're off your duty station."

"No, Sir … the orders have been rescinded."

"By what authority?"

"Yours, Sir."

He ordered me into his office. I reported at once. Now he ordered me "at ease" and to produce evidence. I presented the cash, and a copy of the receipt. He and I counted it, to the penny, and he agreed. Then he told me, "See. Lieutenant, the Army has means of accomplishing much. You need to know how to cut thru the BS and get things done."

It was a valuable lesson. I am to this day grateful for having had the opportunity to serve under a fine officer, who shortly thereafter was promoted to O4, major. He had mentored me in much that is today part and parcel of my managerial fiber.

Michael Toia

QBF

As a radio amateur, or 'ham' radio operator, I once spent a good deal of time on MARS. Not the planet ... the Military Affiliated Radio Service, a system where radio hams voluntarily participate in military communication training. We learned a good bit about establishing and operating radio networks, standard military communications protocols and, in the process, relayed many, many short messages to and from armed forces personnel overseas and their families, free of cost. It was then the day before communication satellites, and decades before the world-wide-web and cell phones. MARS was, at the time, a valuable service.

November and December were really very busy months, with tons of holiday greetings being passed over the networks. One evening, at a pile of short Christmas messages stacked on my radio desk needing forwarding, and in communication with a good friend, the procedures began. We started a run through the workload. My chum, with radio call sign A3NUF, was one of the few amateurs permitted to enter the MARS transcontinental relay networks. His Morse code speed was easily fifty words per minute, the minimum required to enter the transcontinental nets. Mine was a scant thirty-five. His skill had been acquired by his days spent as an NCO at the Army, later USAF, overseas relay station, Goose Bay, Labrador. I was yet in my late teens and learning the practice, and restricted to the statewide networks.

The statewide nets operated both in voice and Morse, our preference that evening being the latter. Standard protocol employed short abbreviations, many of them three-letter, so-called 'Q' and 'Z' signals. These are similar to the 'ten-four' and such used by police and CB radio operators. He had transmitted 'QSG 5,' whose meaning was, and yet is, "Send messages five at a time, and I will roger for them as a group," a fairly standard protocol. Our stations also allowed "full break in." I could interrupt while his telegraph key was "open," between dits and dahs (dots and dashes) if need be, by just hitting a few short "dits" on my telegraph key. He would pause, and I could ask for a repeat of a missing word or two. Though this action was bilateral, I was the one using it; he never missed a beat. The QSG procedure expedited message transmission considerably.

Knowing this, and sifting through the stack of messages on my operating bench, I began transmitting at my top speed, about thirty-five words per minute. During one run of five messages, my wrist developed a cramp, and no matter how I touched the key, out came gibberish. So I managed to pound out, 'AS AS,' the two letters run together as a single burst, the signal to "wait."

While I shook out my wrist, he shot back, "INT QBF." INT, short for interrogation, is the code for a query rather than an answer, but that specific 'Q' signal was unfamiliar. So, while tapping out an occasional 'AS,' I grabbed for my 'Q/Z' signal code book in the bottom desk drawer, thumbed quickly through its pages and looked it up. It was in the subgroup of 'Q' signals of WWII related to aircraft operations

The meaning? 'ARE YOU FLYING IN CLOUD?'

He, a retired USAF communications sergeant of WWII, used this to 'jab' me kiddingly, asking if I was having trouble seeing my own message text because of fog.

A3NUF, Bill, was one of my mentor troupe, a grand gentleman to whom I owe a lot.

A/N-BBB-1

V-J Day arrived. World War II ended. I was but a youth of seven and quickly became interested in electronics. The patient coaching of my father and a few neighborhood elders led to attainment of an amateur radio, or ham license. Although electronic equipment can be expensive, the end of the war produced copious amounts of high-quality, low cost Army Surplus equipment. Along with much else, radio transmitters, receivers, and assorted related equipment flooded the market, endowing many a ham radio station. My first was no exception.

That equipment was wonderfully constructed, and employed the very latest in the state-of-the-art designs developed especially for the war effort. They were marvels of electronics and mechanics, with knobs, gears, tubes, bundles of neatly laced wiring, and on, and on. Many of them carried a brass nameplate identifying the item, often with the additional note, "Signal Corps Engineering Laboratory, Ft. Monmouth, New Jersey." That note piqued my interest, and kindled a dream, an urge, to become a member of the Fort Monmouth laboratory team, and on my graduation from college a decade later as a new, young scientist, the dream was fulfilled.

The laboratory engagement was interrupted by a two-year service period in the Army Signal Corps, followed by a return to the former employment. In those precious years, there occurred exposure to all sorts of Army communications equipment, whether radio, telephone, radar, power generators, and what-not. It was learned that military electronic systems are quite often identified using an "Army-Navy Standard" nomenclature system. The first two letters of equipment's moniker begin with 'A/N' followed by a dash. Then came three additional letters, another dash, and a sort of sequence number to distinguish one system from another. Designations such as "A/N-PRC-24, A/N-GRC-9," and the like are familiar to many of the Korean or Vietnam War era vets.

The first letter following 'A/N-' indicated the equipment's intended environment: A for aircraft, G for ground based, P for man-pack, etc. The second indicated its technical family: R for radio, T for telephone, and so on. The third indicated the equipment's purpose: C for communication, T for transmitting, R for receiving, L for special purpose, and the like. For example, an A/N-TRC-24 was a "Transportable, Radio, Communication" system, the A/N-PRC-6 a "Portable, Radio, Communication" device, the walkie-talkie of Korean and Vietnam War time; and on it went.

History had by now marched on to 1960. The gang at the Fort Monmouth Signal Laboratories ginned up the following gag, theoretically possible, designation, the A/N-BBB-1. Having joked about the lunch table rather consistently on the matter, all decided, that of any possible combination of the three letters, this was by far the most ridiculous, silly, and impossible combination: B for environment, B for family, and B for purpose – the *Underwater Pigeon Bomber*, first such device.

Yes, at one time the Army did have a pigeon service, employing carrier pigeons to carry messages, but apparently dropped that line of equipment, for by the mid-60s the second B was dropped, and possibly reassigned. My guess is they had eaten the last carrier pigeon somewhere in Korea a few years earlier.

Angry

A Dilbert video clip jocularly defines an engineer as one possessing "an exceptional intuition into all things mechanical and electrical, with related social ineptitudes." There are many in possession of this double-edged sword, a combination gift/curse, a part of their very being. A young boy, our subject in this story, suffered so, fumbling socially at school and elsewhere while disassembling any piece of discarded machinery that fell to his hands, observing how the various gears, belts, shafts, vacuum tubes, wires, and assorted other parts complemented each other, forming a whole far more than the simple sum of its parts. I, too, am so blessed and cursed. This tale could well have been mine.

The boy grew, ever curious, always interested, learning anything he could about those fascinating devices, asking of his elders explanations of what he did not yet know. And, he grew in knowledge. As a young teen, he took the nearly obligatory step into ham radio, guided by his father, the town's elder engineers, scientists, and workers in the radio art, building from plans in handbooks and science magazines his radio station, improving upon it as years ticked by.

He became a young man.

Mother and father, noting his keen interest in this area, sent him to college. Though they were far from wealthy, they scraped together what was necessary, sacrificing as need be, and the young man became further and formally educated as an engineer, graduated, and found himself a Lieutenant in the US Army Signal Corps by way of the Reserve Officers' Training Corps. Off he went to his active duty assignment, a two-year conscription into a signal company at a post in a distant state. He retained and continued to build his skills through that interest in ham radio, and met several similar young radio ham peer and higher officers in the Signal Group of two battalions, one the parent of three companies, his included.

Our lad had had a bit of trouble in college. He took employment to work his way through, and required two calendar years to complete his senior year, graduating a year later than his comrades, and a year older. Further, his call to duty was delayed considerably, so in the Signal Group he was about two years older than the average Lieutenant and, hence, a tad more mature and adult. This worked to his advantage. His knowledge of the subject matter was a small, demonstrable bit ahead of that of the others. The organization of the Signal group called for a fixed number of officers skilled in the radio and communications arts, and in the six or so companies of two battalions, a single position as a radio repair and maintenance officer. Our lad was assigned this title, and became the group's sole such officer.

It was proper. He was sought out for his learned knowledge and, to some, advanced skill at diagnosing problems in malfunctioning equipment and directing its repair. He established a good rapport with both the officer corps and the troops under his leadership, having been taught his first management skills in basic officers' school. This education he took to heart, particularly the admonition that an officer is responsible, among all other things, for the accomplishment of the mission and the welfare of his men. For there is too much work for one person to do, and the men under his leadership will do the work, but are his prime asset and tool, and are to be cared for at just about all costs.

There came a field exercise. Our young officer found himself in charge of a complicated bit of communications equipment housed

Michael Toia

in a semi-trailer van – a telephone switchboard, the old fashioned plug-and jack type, a good deal larger but similar to Earnestine, the telephone operator's device of the Laugh-In show fame. It was not at all radio related. All his maintenance tools, equipment, spare parts, had, on purpose, been left behind at the home base. There were other companies in the exercise that cared for radio maintenance during the two-month field maneuver.

On a particular day he was summoned forth, to the company operations tent. The CO, as company commanders were called, asked, "Lieutenant, do you know anything about the transmitter in an Angry-26?"

The Angry-26, as many signalmen will attest, was a standard radio communications unit with a reasonably powerful transmitter. Hundreds were built – perhaps thousands.

The Lieutenant answered. And the following conversation occurred:

Lt.: "Which model, sir? They run from A through H, and the transmitters differ."

CO: "You're familiar with them?"

Lt.: "I've worked with them all."

And, it was true. These were very popular, and our man had, indeed, worked on all, either in school or in various military MARS stations during his college and short pre-military career.

CO: "There's an Angry-26 at this position."

He pointed to a map on an easel.

"My driver will take you there. Its transmitter is inoperative. See what you can do."

Lt.: "With what, sir? My teeth and fingernails? We have no test gear or tools here in the field."

CO: "I'm aware of that. But you're a radio repair and maintenance officer. Take a look. See if you can figure out what the problem is."

With that, the Lieutenant was dismissed in the company of the CO's driver, and by jeep traveled the ten or so miles to the designated map coordinates. As they approached, a young sergeant in charge of the site came to attention and saluted, the salute was returned, with an "At ease!" command. Lieutenant and the sergeant chatted a bit.

Lt.: "What's the problem?

Sgt.: "When we tune up the transmitter, all goes well until we hit the high voltage switch. Then a circuit breaker pops and shuts down the power."

Lt.: "Go ahead. Tune up. Get it operating."

Sgt.: "It's useless, sir. It won't work."

Lt.: "Do it anyway."

And, as the sergeant went through the several steps, the lieutenant observed and took notes. He evaluated whether the sergeant was familiar with the equipment and, indeed, the sergeant did everything properly, short of hitting the last switch.

Lt.: "Hit the switch."

Sgt.: "The circuit breaker will pop."

Lt.: "Hit it anyway."

As the sergeant did so, the circuit breaker popped, with a bit of a snap of a short circuit.

Lt.: "What do you think is wrong?"

Sgt.: "I'm not sure, sir."

Lt.: "Did you look inside the PA compartment?"

The PA, or final power amplifier, is a large radio tube with associated parts. It uses high voltage and amplifies the radio signal to several hundred watts. It occupied a portion of the transmitter on the top left side of the overall metal cabinetry.

Lt.: "Do you know how to look?"

Sgt.: "Yes, sir. Just lift this small door on the top of the transmitter."

The sergeant opened the door. The parts inside looked normal. Nothing inside appeared damaged or burned in any manner. So, the diagnosis continued.

> Lt.: "Get the Jesus stick."

> Sgt.: "Jesus stick, sir?"

Now they were getting somewhere. They had run into the upper limit of the sergeant's knowledge of his equipment, which had been the lieutenant's objective through their interaction to this point. The sergeant's education had been evaluated, and was quite good. It was now time to switch to instructor/student mode.

> Lt.: "Have a good-sized screwdriver?"

> Sgt.: "Yes, sir, in the toolbox."

And he procured the tool.

> Lt.: "Go behind the transmitter. Turn off the main circuit breaker. Begin removing the screws holding the rear panel in place. Remove the panel. Save the screws."

Now the rear panel was removed and set aside.

> Lt.: "Look at the very bottom, rear of the chassis."

There, attached with two large clips, was a brown plastic rod-type device, about two feet long, with a metal hook extending from one end. The sergeant was instructed to detach it. As he pulled it forth, the other end was seen to be attached to a thin braided metal belt several feet long, and the belt unfolded as the device was removed. The belt's other end was firmly bolted to the metal chassis.

> Lt.: "That is the Jesus stick. It's used to probe high voltage points before you reach inside with your hand, to assure that the voltage is off. The first time it actually does its intended function and short-circuits a high voltage, you'll hear a loud snap and see a good spark. Jesus will be the first person you'll think of, and you'll thank Him."

The lieutenant took the Jesus stick. The two stepped around to the front of the unit. The lieutenant poked the stick inside the PA compartment, and touched its metal hook to a large metal cap affixed to the top of the big radio tube. There was neither noise nor spark. Rather, the cap moved. It should not have. Something was amiss. The glass of the big tube had cracked neatly just below the metal cap, leaving the structure inside the tube dangling from the loose cap, and admitting air. This vacuum tube was no more.

Lt.: "Sergeant. Do you see what's happening?"

Sgt.: "The cap is loose. The tube is broken?"

Lt.: "Yep. And all of its vacuum got out. So, all you need do is put the vacuum back inside and patch the crack. If I send you a can of vacuum, can you do the job?"

The sergeant was silent. What was he saying? It sounded preposterous. But, he's a superior officer. I can't just insult him!

Lt.: "A joke, sergeant. That's not a field repairable maneuver. The tube is dead. It needs to be replaced. Do you know how?"

Sgt.: "Yes, sir."

Lt.: "You should have a spare on board. Do you?"

Sgt.: "No, sir. It wasn't there when we checked out and signed for this equipment."

Lt.: "Okay. Go ahead and remove the broken tube."

The lieutenant watched as the sergeant did so, and became satisfied that the sergeant and his two-man crew knew the proper procedures to effect a repair. The lieutenant then further instructed the sergeant and his crew, showing the broken tube, and pointing out what causes such failures and how to avoid them. It is simply a matter of careless operation and allowing the thing to seriously overheat, causing the glass to crack.

With that the lieutenant took his leave, the sergeant saluted and it was returned. The lieutenant then shook his hand, and said, "Well done."

Oh, yes…The lieutenant returned to base, reported the problem, and his counterpart lieutenant and close friend, the supply officer, had two such tubes at the transmitter in three hours. ***Three hours?***

The transmitter was back on the air, and our lad marveled at how his colleague could get supplies to the field so rapidly!

Frank

A deep interest in radio served well over the years. While pursuing a bachelor's degree in engineering, application was made, an exam taken and passed, and a government-issued commercial radiotelephone license earned. This opened the door to employment possibilities. A major radio station had need of a summer replacement to accommodate their staff engineers' vacation schedules. The position was as a studio engineer, controlling the flow of programming. The station, a bit shorthanded, offered employment through the end of December.

Broadcast format was along the lines of easy listening, local and national news interjected on an hourly cycle, and occasional pre-recorded interviews with various radio celebrities. The station had its contingent of DJs, producing and airing their individual shows. This was my first job as an engineer of sorts, becoming initiated into the field, learning and enjoying the process while earning a bit to pay for college expenses. I was young, and on the staff was another young starter-upper, a deejay named Frank. His show ran between 10 P.M. and 2 A.M, when the station went off-the-air until 6 A.M. My shift was 9 P.M. until 5 A.M, the last three hours devoted to routine maintenance following a daily schedule produced by the station's chief engineer.

In the 2 to 5 A.M. time period, Frank retired to the station's large library of vinyl LP records, the high-quality format of that day. He composed his shows for the coming few evenings. And at 5 A.M, we ended our duties for that shift, departed together, then found our way to *Mama Rosa's*, an all-night restaurant. We enjoyed a hearty breakfast of good, Italian fare – a large helping of spaghetti with sausage or meatballs, sometimes lasagna, and each other's company, then departed for our homes about the time the city began its daily stirrings. We became close friends

College studies concluded the following June, the bachelor's degree conferred, and on the last day of December a beautiful young lady named Joyce had agreed to, and did, become my bride and the joy of my life. She was Joy. Together we departed for another state where employment was offered me, now a fully accredited engineer in electronics. Over the next several years we traveled about a bit, following an obligation to serve in the military, and then on to other engineering positions with advancing salary. Our home, the place we were reared and the center of our extended family remained back at the city served by that broadcast station. We returned and visited a few times each year.

Frank's career also proceeded, he remaining a deejay and radio personality, growing in stature and fame on the local stations. A decade had passed from our initial meeting. We had not kept in touch.

Joyce and I visited the family as guests of her parents, occupying her former room. Christmas had passed, the New Year approached. One evening she, her mother, and I were thinking of retiring for the night, listening to a radio show on a local station. The midnight news came, ended, and a familiar voice announced, "This is Frank Tomascello bringing you the news and more easy listening music."

"Frank," I said, "why, he and I worked together years ago. I'll be doggoned."

Mom said, "You know him?" a bit of awe in her voice. "He's a famous radio announcer. Do you think he'd remember you?"

Well, I really couldn't say. It had been a decade plus. But, as both wife and mother continued their bit of excitement, there was one way to find out. Call the station, and so the call was placed.

A voice answered, "WWSW radio." I didn't recognize it, said I was a former colleague of Frank, gave my name, and asked if I might speak with him. At the time a recording of music was being broadcast. There was a gap of a few moments where he might speak to me.

The voice continued. "Mike! Good gosh! I hadn't heard from you in years. How are you doing? Do you think you could meet me after my shift about 1 A.M. at Mama Rosa's?"

It *was* Frank. He sounded so different "off mic" without the station's acoustics and electronic audio processing. I asked him to wait a second, turned to the living room company, and asked, "Ya wanna drive into town and have breakfast with Frank?"

Mom was quite impressed, but tired, so begged off. But Joyce said, "Well, sure! Let's go!"

So, I continued with Frank, got last-minute details, arranged to meet him at the appointed time, and off we went, on a midnight jaunt to the city some fifteen miles distant.

Mama Rosas's was still there, right in downtown, hadn't changed a bit as far as I could tell. Frank was already inside, spotted us, stood, and waved us to his table. He had never met Joyce, so introductions were completed, and we settled down to a bit of Italian fare and lots of chatter … reminiscing chatter. How we had worked together those early years. How we had found Mama Rosas's. The scores of paper airplanes we sailed out of the fourteenth story window of the station's former studios during long runs of taped music or other network programming. How Joyce and I had met, some of our experiences, and a good update on Frank's career progression.

We went well into and through the wee hours, lost track of time, consumed a few pots of coffee, put on a few pounds. Then Frank glanced at his watch. "Good Lord! Look at the time! I need to be out in the eastern 'burbs in an hour, and promised the transmitter crew I would bring them a carton of cigarettes when I stopped by the house to freshen up. But home is ten miles Northwest, near the transmitter, and I just can't make it. How am I going to apologize to them?"

We came to a compromise. I had been reared almost in the air hazard lights of the station's towers, but had never had the opportunity to visit for a look-see. I told Frank that Joyce and I would be glad to deliver the cigarettes; we agreed, and in short order we bade one another farewell, parted company, he driving eastbound, and we, northwest, following the few instructions Frank had scribbled on a napkin.

An hour or so before dawn, with the area under a cover of a few inches of snow, a bit of ground fog had formed. The main road was relatively clear, but as we made our last turn down Cemetery Lane, it became more opaque. We noticed the lane was well named – we were, indeed, driving through a cemetery! The scene was one from a B-grade spooky movie. We came to the lane's end. The fog took on a faint, blinking red glow from the hazard lights of the radio towers. We found the transmitter building.

I said, "Stay in the car. I'll go see if we can get in. Wait for me, I'll wave when you should come, then turn off the headlights and come ahead." Joyce agreed. She waited. I walked to the obvious entranceway, knocked, and waited. No response. I knocked again, louder. The door began to open ... slowly ... and a curious face peered out into the fog, into the darkness, dispelled a bit by the headlights, then focused on me.

Now a bit of background need be injected to appreciate the full impact of that instant in history. Joyce and I worked at the time in Washington, DC, at the same government facility, the Federal Communications Commission. As the scene was eerily spooky, very early in the morning, I wanted to assure the transmitter crew would, indeed, admit us, not for an official visit, other than to fulfill a promise made to my good friend, and as a simple tour to see the facility. I had taken from my jacket pocket my identification folder, containing a photo of myself, the Commission's seal, and the all-important wording identifying me as an engineer of the FCC with the phrase, "His authority shall not be questioned."

As the face focused on me, I said, "Federal Communications Commission! Open the door!"

The poor chap about fainted, but he did as commanded. I said, "Just a moment. My secretary is here, as well." I waved to Joyce. We entered the facility. I then met the other attendant on duty, asked for a short inspection visit, looked over the large transmitter, glanced intently at its various meters and settings, and then asked that we all sit down somewhere to talk. The two on duty led us to their office/cubicle. We took seats, and I continued while Joyce smiled slightly, courteously, and professionally.

"I'm an FCC engineer, and the two of us are natives of the area. I've grown up almost in the lights of your towers, and had always wanted to see this place. Thank you so much for the opportunity at last. This is not an official FCC inspection, though such is within my authority. Actually, I am a personal friend of Frank Tomascello, and just had breakfast with him. We lost track of time, reminiscing about our former years together. He promised you cigarettes, but got in a terrible time crunch, so we volunteered to do him a favor." I turned to Joyce, who held a paper bag, took the bag as she handed it to me, removed the carton, and handed it to the two.

They were still in a bit of shock, didn't say a whole lot, but with that we took our leave, thanked them again, returned to the car, and began our drive back to Joyce's girlhood home. Dawn was breaking. We got back, a bit of sleep, and had a good story for mom at breakfast. As for the transmitter crew's well-being? They say cigarettes are bad for your health. Possibly so. They're called coffin nails, and we had driven through a cemetery.

Compass

Ed was a hard-working, amazing engineer. He recruited me to be part of his team. We spent quite a bit of time at a large field test site a few hours drive from home, near a small city. The work was deeply interesting and quite engaging, the type that causes a day to fly past without notice. Often we worked well past suppertime, then retired to a local restaurant to end the evening.

It became January ... the weather turned cold ... dark fell early. And, on one of those field trips, a light, cold rain set in. It was another long day, running well past suppertime. Finally work was done, and the crew voted on where to get food and have a few beers.

Ed and I were from out of town, and did not know the local area well. A few contractors working with us did. They recommended a pizza parlor, and it was decided – pizza and beer for the evening. Instructions on finding the place were a bit elaborate, as the city had many one-way streets. The contractors' crew left in a lead vehicle, followed by Ed in his auto and I in mine.

Apparently the contractors were not as familiar with the route as they thought, or the darkness and rain caused confusion. We traveled quite a way, took a few wrong turns, and then stopped at a gas station mini-mart to ask for directions. We were way off track, but armed with better information, finally reached our target.

Ambiance was ideal for the purpose, a nice blue-collar working man's place, good pizza, good beer, and good company. We ate. We drank. We talked and joked around a bit. We enjoyed the company and the night. But, all good things must end, as did that evening. We exited the establishment, and had a final evening farewell in the parking lot.

Ed and I were not even aware of where we were in relation to our motel. We discussed how to get there with the contract crew. As so many of the streets were one-way, they gave us somewhat involved directions: "Turn left out of the parking lot. At the second street turn left. Go three blocks and turn right. In one more block turn left, then take the ramp onto the state highway. Go three miles, exit right, cross a railroad, turn left. Motel is on the right ... you can't miss it." Famous last words.

This was the final take of instructions. Some of the contractor crew suggested alternate routes, which did nothing but confuse the matter further. As we rehearsed these instructions, Ed asked, "Does anyone have a compass?" This added a good bit of levity to the conversation, helped along by the recently imbibed beer. I have to admit, Ed's comment was an ideal punch line to a good joke. Everyone laughed. Ed, too, was rather jocular about it.

As the instructions were rehearsed, Ed continued his, "Does anyone have a compass?" comment. It was a good joke at first, and became all the more humorous with several repeats during the instruction session.

Finally, the contractors took their leave and drove off. Ed and I stood in the parking lot under a street light, the light cold rain falling, both confused about how to find our motel and exactly where we were. Because of the devious route of approach, we could not begin to retrace our way back to the test site. We were truly lost.

Then Ed said, "What's wrong with those guys? I want a compass."

This just got me to laughing a bit harder, until he said, "What's so funny? I'm serious. I want a compass." I said, "Really? I thought you were joking." With that I reached into my briefcase and pulled therefrom a Silva map compass that I usually carry. I presented it.

Ed said, "Finally! Someone listens to me."

Now you won't believe this, but it's the truth. The two of us, senior engineers with our firm, each with several decades of experience under our belts, stood there, looked at that compass under the street light, and neither could decide if the RED end or WHITE end of the needle pointed north!

Printed in the USA
CPSIA information can be obtained
at www.ICGtesting.com
CBHW071226210524
8690CB00017BA/110